GREAT LIVES OBSERVED

Gerald Emanuel Stearn, *General Editor*

EACH VOLUME IN THE SERIES VIEWS THE CHARACTER AND ACHIEVEMENT OF A GREAT WORLD FIGURE IN THREE PERSPECTIVES—THROUGH HIS OWN WORDS, THROUGH THE OPINIONS OF HIS CONTEMPORARIES, AND THROUGH RETROSPECTIVE JUDGMENTS—THUS COMBINING THE INTIMACY OF AUTOBIOGRAPHY, THE IMMEDIACY OF EYEWITNESS OBSERVATION, AND THE OBJECTIVITY OF MODERN SCHOLARSHIP.

STANLEY I. KUTLER, *editor of this volume in the Great Lives Observed series, is Professor of History at the University of Wisconsin. He is the author of* Judicial Power and Reconstruction Politics, The Supreme Court and the Constitution, *and* Privilege and Creative Destruction.

GREAT LIVES OBSERVED

JOHN MARSHALL

GREAT LIVES OBSERVED

John Marshall

Edited by **STANLEY I. KUTLER**

> *We must never forget that*
> *it is a constitution we are expounding.*
> —JOHN MARSHALL
> McCulloch *v.* Maryland, 1819

> *America has chosen to be, in many respects,*
> *and to many purposes, a nation;*
> *and for all these purposes her government is complete;*
> *to all these objects, it is competent.*
> —JOHN MARSHALL
> Cohens *v.* Virginia, 1821

A SPECTRUM BOOK

PRENTICE-HALL, INC., ENGLEWOOD CLIFFS, N.J.

Library of Congress Cataloging in Publication Data

KUTLER, STANLEY I   COMP.
    John Marshall.

    (Great lives observed) (A Spectrum book)
    Bibliography: p.
    1. Marshall, John, 1755–1835.
KF8745.M3K85   347'.73'2634 [B]   72–6101
ISBN 0–13–510271–5
ISBN 0–13–510263–4 (pbk.)

© 1972 by PRENTICE-HALL, INC.
Englewood Cliffs, New Jersey

A SPECTRUM BOOK

10 9 8 7 6 5 4 3 2 1

Printed in the United States of America

PRENTICE-HALL INTERNATIONAL, INC. (*London*)
PRENTICE-HALL OF AUSTRALIA, PTY. LTD. (*Sydney*)
PRENTICE-HALL OF CANADA, LTD. (*Toronto*)
PRENTICE-HALL OF INDIA PRIVATE LIMITED (*New Delhi*)
PRENTICE-HALL OF JAPAN, INC. (*Tokyo*)

For Bob and Carolyn Sachs

CONTENTS

Introduction

"The events of my life are too unimportant, and have too little interest for any person not of my immediate family, to render them worth communicating or preserving." So wrote John Marshall in 1827 in an autobiographical sketch prepared for his friend and colleague, Joseph Story. It was a rare understatement and certainly altogether too modest. From 1801 to 1835, Marshall presided over the United States Supreme Court, lending grace, dignity, and above all, authority to an institution only vaguely endowed with power by the Constitution and often disdainfully regarded by contemporaries. His opinions shaped constitutional law, greatly affecting developments in his own time and, more significantly, the future course of American history. Perhaps as much as those of any prominent American historical figure, his contributions have had an enduring and ever-relevant impact on the nation's life and government. Marshall was not the first chief justice of the United States, but surely he must forever be known as the "great chief justice."

Marshall's contributions as chief justice cannot be separated from his activities before he came to the high bench. The events of American history and politics prior to 1801, and Marshall's relationship to them, decisively shaped his future outlook on the Supreme Court. He was born in 1755 in the proverbial log cabin in Fauquier County on the Virginia frontier and raised in a large, close-knit family. His mother belonged to the prominent Randolph family, and through her, Marshall was related to Thomas Jefferson. His father, Thomas Marshall, profoundly influenced him; "he was," as Marshall later wrote, "my only intelligent companion; and was both a watchfull parent and an affectionate instructive friend." Thomas Marshall supervised his son's early education, basically relying on Pope's essays and poetry. At fourteen, John was sent for a year to Westmoreland County, a hundred miles away, to study with the Reverend Archibald Campbell. After his return, he studied the classics with a tutor at home and English literature with his father. Thomas Marshall subscribed to the first American publication (in 1772) of Blackstone's *Commentaries,* and probably at this time, John

1

began his self-training in the law. His father's political interests also undoubtedly contributed to the younger Marshall's development. In the fifteen years prior to the outbreak of the Revolution, Thomas Marshall successively served as a delegate to the Virginia House of Burgesses, sheriff of Fauquier County, clerk for Dunmore County, and principal vestryman for his parish. More important, he closely allied himself with Patrick Henry and the early revolutionary leaders in the colony, and he was a friend and admirer of his former employer, George Washington. Shortly after the skirmishes with British troops at Lexington and Concord, the Marshalls trained a militia force gathered from among their neighbors.

The American Revolution laid the basis for Marshall's strong sense of national union. Years later, he claimed that it "confirmed [me] in the habit of considering America as my country and Congress as my government." He was appointed first lieutenant in the Culpeper Minutemen, in the summer of 1775, and by autumn, he had seen action against Lord Dunmore's troops at Greatbridge and during the British siege of Norfolk. A few weeks after the Declaration of Independence, Marshall joined the Continental Army as a first lieutenant in the Eleventh Virginia Regiment. Subsequently promoted to captain, he distinguished himself at the battles of Brandywine, Germantown, Monmouth, and Stony Point. After his regiment's enlistment expired in 1779, he returned to Virginia to await a new command. He resumed active duty only briefly in October 1780, however, and resigned his commission in February 1781. During his leave in 1780, Marshall attended the law lectures offered by the distinguished chancellor, George Wythe, at the College of William and Mary, and in August of that year, he was admitted to the bar in Fauquier County. Such was his "formal" legal training.

Following his separation from the army, Marshall's political, personal, and professional fortunes blossomed. In 1782, his Fauquier neighbors elected him to the legislature, necessitating a move to Richmond, where he established his law practice. There he met and married Mary Willis Ambler, daughter of the state treasurer. The alliance strengthened the ties of kinship that were so important to the politics of the day.

Marshall's legislative experience, together with his wartime service, decisively fixed his commitment to the necessity for strong, effective national government. During his first term in the assembly, he also served as a member of the Executive Council and acquired intimate experience with the typical questions of the day, such as paper money, maintenance of public order, and collection of taxes. At this time, according to his autobiographical statement, Marshall's political opinions were "tinctured" with "wild and enthusiastic democracy." The events of the 1780s, however, changed his outlook permanently. His legislative service, he later wrote, and the "general tendency" of state politics, convinced him of the need for a more efficient, better organized national government, along with restrictions on the powers of state governments. But for Marshall, as well as for other prominent figures of the period, Shays' Rebellion in Massachusetts with its bitter debtor-creditor conflict left a lasting imprint. That insurrection, he commented in 1787, "cast a deep shade over that bright prospect which the revolution in America and the establishment of our free governments had opened to the votaries of liberty throughout the globe." Perhaps after all, he continued, "man is incapable of governing himself." His pessimism was complete: "I fear," he concluded, "we may live to see another revolution."

Marshall's perception of the United States under the Articles of Confederation never changed; he constantly reiterated it in his major constitutional opinions as chief justice, and it recurred regularly as a theme in his monumental *Life of George Washington*. The ineptitude of the national government and the threat of anarchy stayed with him as constant reminders of the need for strong, effective authority. For Marshall, the constitution resulting from the Philadelphia deliberations in 1787 promised a viable remedy.

Marshall played a prominent role in Virginia in support of the Constitution. As a member of the legislature, he consistently had backed James Madison's efforts to secure a new agreement with the other states. Representing the city of Richmond in 1787, he led the drive to call a convention to ratify the document drafted in Philadelphia. In the process, Marshall and his nationalist allies barely beat down attempts to saddle the convention with designated amendments. Marshall stood for election to the convention from Henrico County, which included Richmond, and where opposition to the proposed new government seemed overwhelming. Marshall's personal popularity, however, carried him to victory, despite Patrick Henry's endorsement of his opponent.

In the convention, Marshall spoke only on a few occasions and

generally emphasized the need for enlarging national power. Ironi-
cally, the pro-constitution forces selected Marshall to defend the
new idea of a national judiciary. Marshall forcefully emphasized
the relationship of an independent judiciary to the maintenance of
liberty and justice. But most important, his comment on judicial
review offers pointed evidence that such power was widely assumed
by proponents of the new constitution. The judiciary, Marshall told
the convention, offered the best protection against infringement on
the Constitution and the rights of the people. Federal judges, he
insisted, were obligated to void any exercise of congressional power
"not warranted by any of the powers enumerated." That statement,
of course, proved as elastic for judicial review as for constitutional
powers.

With the Constitution ratified and the new national administration headed by Washington firmly established in power, Marshall
eagerly sought to return to his lucrative law practice. But politics
still dominated his life. He unstintingly supported the new government and soon emerged as one of the Federalist leaders in Virginia.
Early in the 1790s, he rejected several overtures to run for Congress,
and in 1795, he even declined Washington's offer of the attorney
generalship. But that year, Marshall again was elected to the state
legislature, where, amidst growing opposition to the national government, he defended the Washington administration and the unpopular Jay Treaty. The following year, John Adams unsuccess-
fully offered him appointment as minister to France, but in 1797,
Marshall agreed to serve in the peace mission to France that resulted
in the so-called X.Y.Z. affair. Marshall's motives for joining the
delegation are not entirely clear; in any event, he was well compensated, receiving nearly $20,000 from a very generous Congress.
Apparently, there were even more rewards in store, for Adams
offered the Virginian a seat on the Supreme Court in 1798; but again
Marshall declined.

The same year, however, Washington prevailed upon his young
admirer to run as a Federalist candidate for Congress. Despite the
growing unpopularity of the Federalist party, Marshall retained
enough of a personal following in the Richmond area to win. Last
minute support from Patrick Henry undoubtedly helped his cause.
The controversy over the Alien and Sedition Acts raised the central
issue of the campaign, and Marshall's views underscored his differences with the extremist wing of the Federalist party. He publicly

opposed the laws on the grounds that they were "useless" and that they served to "create unnecessary discontents and jealousies." The extremists were furious. "Our good people all censure Mr. Marshall for his opinions of the Sedition Act," George Cabot reported to Timothy Pickering in 1798. But Marshall refused to follow the party line on the Sedition Act, and after taking his seat, he voted for repeal of the section providing punishment for seditious speech. Marshall, in general, loyally supported the Adams administration, particularly the president's ardent efforts to establish peace with France. His performance only further alienated the "good people."

By 1800, Adams no longer could ignore the dissension within the party and his own administration. He dismissed two cabinet officers —Pickering of State and McHenry of War—and moved to bring Marshall into the executive branch. First, in May, 1800, without consulting Marshall, Adams nominated him for secretary of war, but the Virginian declined. A few weeks later, however, the president prevailed upon Marshall to accept the post of secretary of state.

Marshall's decision to accept executive office in 1800 proved highly significant for future developments, but it also raises a number of questions regarding his motives. After all, Marshall had declined such posts before, including one offered by his hero, George Washington. Furthermore, while he steadfastly supported Adams, they were not intimates, and it is unlikely Marshall agreed to serve merely to comfort a beleaguered president. Why, then, should he join an unpopular, isolated, and dying administration? Perhaps Marshall was more optimistic. Looking about in 1800, a Federalist partisan need not have concluded that his party was in its death throes. That is a judgment of history, supported with the certain knowledge of subsequent events. The party, however, was a going concern in 1800; indeed, it is well to remember that Adams lost to Jefferson by a relatively small margin. Party unity could have spelled the difference between defeat and victory. Although Marshall might have recognized Federalist vitality, he could have seen, nevertheless, that the party's divisions had resulted in a leadership vacuum, and that only one relatively untarnished and uninvolved in the internecine struggle could unite the divergent factions. Virginia, of course, was a crucial state, and by 1800, it had one outstanding Federalist—John Marshall. He had made his mark in local politics, his personal appeal proved strong enough for him to gain a congressional seat, and he had established his prominence as part of the mission to France and in Congress; perhaps in 1800, Marshall believed it was time to climb the executive ladder in pursuit of the ultimate prize. As subsequent presidents proved—Jefferson, Madison, Monroe, and John Quincy Adams—the secretaryship of state was the penultimate rung. All this, naturally, is speculative; furthermore, if it were Marshall's charted direction, John Adams threw him off course with the appointment as chief justice in January, 1801.

Marshall's nomination to the high court, similarly, was entangled in the political machinations of the day. In December, 1800, Chief Justice Oliver Ellsworth resigned because of poor health. Immediately, Adams nominated John Jay, the first chief justice (from 1789 to 1795), to replace Ellsworth. But Adams had done so without consulting the New Yorker, and Jay declined. Adams' enemies within the Federalist party pushed Associate Justice William Paterson and Charles Cotesworth Pinckney; Marshall himself later claimed that he had recommended Paterson to the president. On January 20, 1801, Adams, apparently to everyone's great surprise—including Marshall's—nominated his secretary of state. In his autobiographical account, Marshall related that when the president offered him the post, he "was pleased as well as surprised, and bowed in silence." Some of Adams's Federalist foes in the Senate immediately indicated displeasure with the nomination, but faced with the alternative of an appointment by the despised Jefferson, they confirmed the president's choice on January 27. For some unexplainable reason, whether congenital laxness or genuine doubts about the position, Marshall held off formal acceptance until February 4. In the meantime, he continued to function as secretary of state until the end of the Adams administration on March 4.

For an event that ultimately proved so momentous for the future, Marshall's appointment aroused relatively little comment. Some Federalists grumbled, and Republicans naturally were suspicious and dismayed by Ellsworth's convenient resignation. But compared to their usual vitriolic attacks on Federalist policies, the Republican press was relatively quiescent. The simple fact is that few cared very much who was chief justice, for it had made virtually no difference in the past. Indeed, when John Jay declined reappointment in 1800, he told Adams that he did not believe the Court ever would acquire enough "energy, weight and dignity" to have much effect and influence in the American governmental apparatus. Undoubtedly, Jay was discouraged by the Court's undistinguished history during the first decade of its existence. Following one of its few significant decisions of the 1790s, *Chisholm* v. *Georgia,* the states responded with a constitutional amendment to reverse the Court's ruling. Also, the onerous circuit duties of the justices made a place on the high bench rather unattractive. The prestige and standing of the Court was so low that, in 1795, Jay resigned to become governor of New York. Yet Jay's view was not universally shared. Charles C. Pinckney, probably the leading southern Federalist in 1801, welcomed Marshall's nomination and thought that it came at a most propitious moment. The triumph of the Jeffersonians naturally filled him with alarm, for he believed they would "construe away the energy of our constitution, . . . unnerve our Government, and . . . overthrow that system by which we have risen to our present prosperity." For Pinckney, however, the Supreme Court offered some hope for resistance; he considered it important that the high bench "should be filled by men of elevated talents, sound federal principles and unshaken firmness." Pinckney, apparently, knew his man.

The Supreme Court is a collegial institution and its decisions, as its processes, are collective ones. Historically, it has been composed of from six to ten members, and the places at a given time have been filled by individuals diverse in their political inclinations and intellectual temperaments. As such, it usually is an exaggeration to focus on one man as preeminent and dominant among his colleagues. But Marshall is an exception. Before 1801, the Court usually announced its opinions *seriatim;* accordingly, it often was difficult to discern common ground and cohesive doctrine from the separate opinions. With Marshall's accession to the chief justiceship, however, the Court's procedure changed markedly. Dissents and concurring opinions were rare, as the justices massed their views in a shared opinion usually written by the chief justice himself. Indeed, in over 1200 opinions delivered during Marshall's long tenure, the chief justice spoke for his colleagues nearly half the time. To be sure, Marshall paid a price for the Court's outward unanimity, for occasionally he found it necessary to trim his more ambitious intentions.

Yet it probably is an exaggeration to suggest, as some have, that Marshall fundamentally compromised his doctrines. It hardly was necessary. Until 1830, the Supreme Court largely consisted of like-minded men. The judicial appointments by Jefferson and his successors differed from those of Washington and Adams only in party affiliation, not in ideological and constitutional commitment. The Republican appointees invariably represented the party's moderate wing and rarely found themselves in serious disagreement with the views of their moderate Federalist chief justice. The process, of course, was complementary. Marshall's notable differences with William Johnson, Jefferson's first Court appointee, generally were ones of degree and not of kind. Johnson's opposition to the nullification movement in his native South Carolina, for example, must have appalled any Jeffersonian who thought Johnson would faithfully reflect the states'-rights views of a segment of the party. The significance of the massed Marshall Court cannot be underestimated. Unquestionably, the general agreement projected a purposefulness and coherence that had been sorely lacking under the *seriatim* procedure. From 1801 onward, the Supreme Court spoke to the nation as an institution reflecting the common wisdom of its members, and the net effect substantially increased the impact of the Court's decisions.

Marshall's work and contributions on the Supreme Court are best illustrated by the sampling of opinions that follow. They are arranged into traditional legal-constitutional topics, such as jurisdiction, contract clause, and commerce clause. Such categorization, however, runs the risk of arbitrariness and narrowness. Marshall's opinions regularly transcended the specific legal or constitutional questions to encompass broader political, institutional, social, and economic concerns. Take, for example, the wide-ranging considerations and implications of his ruling in *Fletcher* v. *Peck* (1810). Marshall's opinion in this case is at once possibly the most antiquated and the most relevant of his major constitutional decisions: antiquated in that the leading constitutional issue in the case, the contract clause of the federal Constitution, has not been a significant source of litigation or controversy for nearly a century; and relevant in that it portrays fundamental principles of the federal system, the judicial function, and capital investment in a developing economy.

The case involved the Yazoo land grants conveyed by the Georgia legislature in the 1790s to various groups of speculators. There was nothing unusual here except that the legislators had been bribed—

and found out. In classic fashion, in 1796, the citizenry threw the rascals out and elected a new legislature, which promptly rescinded the grant. Meanwhile, the original grantees had sold off their titles, and despite the repeal, ownership of the land continued to change hands over the next decade. After Congress had assumed jurisdiction over the western Georgia lands, the Yazoo situation ultimately involved the national government, and it produced endless political bickering, which even contributed to a rupture within the Jeffersonian party. The Supreme Court became involved when title-holders challenged the state's repeal of the grant as a violation of the constitutional prohibition against state impairment of contracts.

Marshall and his colleagues unanimously upheld the plaintiff's claims. The chief justice's opinion set forth a number of important principles of constitutional law that have had continuing impact. First, he clearly upheld the supremacy of the Constitution over state laws, by finding that the repeal impaired the sanctity of a contract. This holding required Marshall to assert—in the face of contrary evidence—that public grants, no less than contracts between private persons, were meant to have constitutional protection against state impairment. In addition, Marshall's refusal to explore legislative motivation surrounding the original grant—in this case, the question of bribery—established a basic principle of judicial behavior that has been of no small meaning to the democratic process. Policing the sanctity of the legislative process is a function largely left to the legislature and its constituents. But perhaps the dominant aspect of his opinion involved his discussion and recognition of the interaction between public policy and the private investor.

Certainly, John Marshall, a prominent land speculator himself, sought to protect property interests; and certainly, he reflected basic, deeply felt national beliefs in the sanctity of vested rights. But the term "vested rights" often has a negative, abstract connotation indicating the dead hand of reaction; it conveys, also, a static conception of property and capital that belies the prevailing view of a dynamic, expansive economy. Furthermore, Marshall offered ample evidence throughout his career that property rights had a larger community value and could, on occasion, be subordinated to the community's needs. Marshall's great opinion on the commerce clause in *Gibbons*

v. *Ogden* (1824) and another contract-clause decision, *Providence Bank* v. *Billings* (1830), offer vivid examples of this point. Like other public policy spokesmen of the day, Marshall, in *Fletcher* v. *Peck,* was much more concerned with protecting ventures than holdings. Americans in the nineteenth century faced a land rich with boundless opportunities for material reward and advancement. Nothing threatened the limits of their drives and energies more than the scarcity of capital; nothing, therefore, required greater legal security than the venture capital of the bona fide investor, subject only to the risks and vicissitudes of the market. This entrepreneurial mood found full expression in Marshall's opinion as he vigorously asserted the need to protect the innocent, bona fide investor. He coupled an underlying premise that investment capital was scarce and must not be intimidated with the consideration that America's vast lands would remain an unrealized national treasure if capital investment and development were retarded by a hostile legal and political milieu.

In *Fletcher* v. *Peck,* Marshall satisfied himself that the land claimants had fulfilled the basic Lockean-Blackstonian requirement that their property be "justly earned." Whatever fraudulent conditions surrounded the land grants, the claimants were innocent, bona fide investors who need not suffer for the sins of others. Speaking of the plaintiff, Marshall held that the "concealed defect cannot be set up against him. He has paid his money for a title good at law; he is innocent, whatever may be the guilt of others, and equity will not subject him to the penalties attached to that guilt. All titles would be insecure, and the intercourse between man and man would be very seriously obstructed, if this principle be overturned." This was not a static idealization of vested rights; Marshall implicitly was concerned rather with economic security—with peace and tranquility—for the desirable end of encouraging *more* "intercourse between man and man."

Such notions, moreover, were not the exclusive rationalizations of "reactionary, die-hard" Federalists. James Madison, Albert Gallatin, and Levi Lincoln—surely respectable Jeffersonian Republicans—acting as federal commissioners in the purchase of Georgia's western lands, did "not perceive that those companies [which purchased the 1795 claims] have any equitable claim either for the land or for compensation from the United States"; yet the commissioners hastily and significantly added that compensation be paid in behalf of "the interest of the United States, the tranquility of those who may hereafter inhabit that territory, and various equitable considerations. . . ." The judicial and executive branches of government were merely the instruments for enforcing and advancing economic security, which, in turn, was a stimulant to national development. Other investors, petitioning Congress for compensation of their Georgia claims, spoke of the need for relief from their difficulties and reconciled their interests to those of the nation. Compensation, they said, was necessary to rectify "the immense expenses they have been plunged into . . . ; the sacrifice of capital to raise funds, and the loss of interest sunk with it; the loss, also, of time and credit, from the embarrassments arising from their disappointment, as well as the most precious years of their lives; and the sacrifices of that domestic happiness, which is beyond the power of language to express." Putting aside our own value judgments of the wisdom and aftermath of such policy, the premise, in short, was that if the nation were to prosper, it could ill-afford the loss of such energies and resources—both physical and capital. In that important respect, then, indeed, we were all Federalists, we were all Republicans.

Fletcher v. *Peck* also spotlights the very special functional place of the Supreme Court in the governmental apparatus. For here, as in all his great constitutional opinions, John Marshall underlined the Court's authority as a forum for a continuing commentary on the meaning of the Constitution, and also as a custodian and spokesman for the nation's values. Tempered by his own experiences in the beginning of the young republic (from the Revolution through the adoption of the Constitution), Marshall had real insight into both the purposes and potentialities of the American people. With this insight, he molded judicial power as an instrument for their realization. At all times, the Constitution, with its fundamental principles of liberty and law, served as the vehicle. The people, Marshall said in *Marbury* v. *Madison* (1803), had the "right to establish for their future government, such principles as . . . shall most conduce to their own happiness." But if the Constitution were to "endure for ages to come," those principles and considerations for happiness required constant reconciliation with the demands and needs of a developing, ever-changing society. Such is the experience of American constitutionalism. And for that task, Marshall and his colleagues carved out the Supreme Court's special role. Perhaps, then, in the final analysis, Marshall's greatest legacy lies not with the continuing impact of his particular opinions—substantial as it is—but rather with the institutional purpose that he, above all others, clearly defined and utilized.

Chronology of the Life of John Marshall

1755   Born in a log cabin near Germantown, Virginia.

1769–70   Received formal education at Archibald Campbell's Academy and from a Scottish minister living with the family.

1775–80   Officer during the American Revolution, participating in the battles of Brandywine, Germantown, and Monmouth. Spent winter at Valley Forge with Washington.

1780   Attended legal lectures given by Chancellor George Wythe at the College of William and Mary. Admitted to the Virginia Bar.

1782   Elected to the Virginia House of Delegates from Fauquier County. Served as member of the Executive Council.

1783   Married Mary Willis Ambler in Richmond. Began law practice in Richmond.

1784   Reelected to the House of Delegates.

1785   Chosen city recorder for Richmond.

1787   Reelected to State Assembly from Richmond.

1788   Delegate from Henrico County to Virginia convention that considered ratification of the Constitution of 1787.

1790–96   Active in Federalist party politics in Virginia and staunch supporter of Washington's administration.

1795   Declined Washington's offer of attorney generalship.

1796   Argued his only case before the Supreme Court, *Ware v. Hylton.*

1797–98   Participated in X.Y.Z. negotiations in Paris.

1798   Declined seat on Supreme Court.

1799   Elected to U. S. House of Representatives.

1800   Accepted post as secretary of state after refusing appointment as secretary of war.

1801   Appointed chief justice of the United States.

1802   Opinion in *Marbury* v. *Madison* established basic precedent for judicial review of congressional actions.

1804–7   Published five-volume *Life of George Washington.*

1807   Presided in Aaron Burr's trial for treason.

1810   Decision in *Fletcher* v. *Peck* found a state law unconstitutional under the contract clause of the Constitution.

1819   Opinion in *Dartmouth College* v. *Woodward* extended contract
              clause protection to private corporations.
              McCulloch v. *Maryland* opinion elaborated the theory of
              implied powers and sustained the constitutionality of the
              national bank.

1821   *Cohens* v. *Virginia* established the supremacy of federal courts
              over those of the states.

1824   Opinion in *Gibbons* v. *Ogden* examined the nature of the
              commerce power.

1827   Dissented for the only time in a constitutional law case, in
              Ogden v. *Saunders*, in which the Court upheld a state
              bankruptcy law.

1829–30   Served as member of the Virginia Constitutional Convention
              and opposed expansion of the suffrage.

1833   In *Barron* v. *Baltimore*, Marshall refused to extend protection
              of Bill of Rights against state action.

1835   Died in Philadelphia at the age of 80 from a liver ailment.

PART ONE

JOHN MARSHALL LOOKS AT THE WORLD

1
Autobiography

This autobiographical account is a lean, but incisive, summary of Marshall's life to his appointment as chief justice in 1801. Marshall composed it in the form of a letter to his "highly valued friend" and colleague, Justice Joseph Story, probably sometime in 1827. Story had requested the sketch for background to his review of Marshall's History of the Colonies, *and subsequently, Story extensively used it in a published memoir and in his eulogy of Marshall. The "autobiography" offers Marshall's most complete revelations of his role in the X.Y.Z. affair and of his nomination as chief justice.*[1]

The events of my life are too unimportant, and have too little interest for any person not of my immediate family, to render them worth communicating or preserving. I felt therefore some difficulty in commencing their detail, since the mere act of detailing, exhibits the appearance of attaching consequence to them. . . .

In the spring of 1782 I was elected a member of the legislature; and, in the autumn of the same year was chosen a member of the Executive Council. In January 1783 I was married to Miss Ambler the second daughter of our then Treasurer, and in april 1784 resigned my seat at the Council board in order to return to the bar. In the same month I was again elected a member of the legislature for the county of Fauquier of which I was only a nominal resident

[1] John S. Adams, ed., *An Autobiographical Sketch by John Marshall* . . . (Ann Arbor, Mich.: University of Michigan Press, 1937). Reprinted by permission of The William Clements Library, University of Michigan.

having resided actually in Richmond as a member of the Council. Immediately after the election I established myself in Richmond for the purpose of practicing law in the superior courts of Virginia.

My extensive acquaintance in the army was of great service to me. My numerous military friends, who were dispersed over the state, took great interest in my favour, and I was more successful than I had reason to expect. In April 1787, I was elected into the legislature for the county in which Richmond stands; and though devoted to my profession, entered with a good deal of spirit into the politics of the state. The topics of the day were paper money, the collection of taxes, the preservation of public faith, and the administration of justice. Parties were nearly equally divided on all these interesting subjects; and the contest concerning them was continually renewed. The state of the Confederacy was also a subject of deep solicitude to our statesmen. Mr. James Madison had been for two or three years a leading member of the House of Delegates, and was the parent of the resolution for appointing members to a general Convention to be held at Philadelphia for the purpose of revising the confederation. The question whether a continuance of the Union or a separation of the states was most to be desired was some times discussed; and either side of the question was supported without reproach. Mr. Madison was the enlightened advocate of Union and of an efficient federal government; but was not a member of the legislature when the plan of the constitution was proposed to the states by the General Convention. It was at first favorably received; but Mr. P. Henry, Mr. G. Mason, and several other gentlemen of great influence were much opposed to it, and permitted no opportunity to escape of inveighing against it and of communicating their prejudices to others. In addition to state jealousy and state pride, which operated powerfully in all the large states, there were some unacknowledged motives of no inconsiderable influence in Virginia. In the course of the session, the unceasing efforts of the enemies of the constitution made a deep impression; and before its close, a great majority showed a decided hostility to it. I took an active part in the debates on this question and was uniform in support of the proposed constitution.

When I recollect the wild and enthusiastic democracy with which my political opinions of that day were tinctured, I am disposed to ascribe my devotion to the union, and to a government competent to its preservation, at least as much to casual circumstances as to judgement. I had grown up at a time when a love of union and resistance to the claims of Great Britain were the inseparable inmates of the same bosom;—when patriotism and a strong fellow feeling with our suffering fellow citizens of Boston were identical;—when the maxim "united we stand, divided we fall" was the maxim of every orthodox American; and I had imbibed these sentiments so thoughroughly [sic] that they constituted a part of my being. I carried them with me into the army where I found myself associated with brave men from different states who were risking life and everything valuable in a common cause believed by all to be most precious; and where I was confirmed in the habit of considering America as my country, and congress as my government. I partook largely of the sufferings and feelings of the army, and brought with me into civil life an ardent devotion to its interests. My immediate entrance into the state legislature opened to my view the causes which had been chiefly instrumental in augmenting those sufferings, and the general tendency of state politics convinced me that no safe and permanent remedy could be found but in a more efficient and better organized general government. The questions too, which were perpetually recurring in the state legislatures, and which brought annually into doubt principles which I thought most sound, which proved that everything was afloat, and that we had no safe anchorage ground, gave a high value in my estimation to that article in the constitution which imposes restrictions on the states. I was consequently a determined advocate for its adoption, and became a candidate for the convention to which it was to be submitted.

The county in which I resided was decidedly antifederal, but I was at that time popular, and parties had not yet become so bitter as to extinguish the private affections.

A great majority of the people of Virginia was antifederal; but in several of the counties most opposed to the adoption of the constitution, individuals of high character and great influence came forward as candidates and were elected from personal motives. After an ardent and eloquent discussion to which justice never has been and never can be done, during which the constitution was adopted by nine states, the question was carried in the affirmative by a majority of eight voices.

I felt that those great principles of public policy which I considered as essential to the general happiness were secured by this measure & I willingly relinquished public life to devote myself to my profession. Indeed the county was so thoroughly antifederal, & parties had become so exasperated, that my election would have been doubtful. This however was not my motive for withdrawing from the legislature. My practice had become very considerable, and I could not spare from its claims on me so much time as would be necessary to maintain such a standing in the legislature as I was desirous of preserving. . . .

In December 1788 the legislature passed an act allowing a representative to the city of Richmond, and I was almost unanimously invited to become a candidate. The city was federal. I yielded to the general wish partly because a man changes his inclination after retiring from public life, partly because I found the hostility to the government so strong in the legislature as to require from its friends all the support they could give it, and partly because the capitol was then completed, and the courts and the legislature sat in the same building, so that I could without much inconvenience [leave?] the bar to take part in any debate in which I felt a particular interest.

I continued in the assembly for the years 1789 & 1790 & 1791, during which time almost every important measure of the government was discussed, and the whole funding system was censured; that part of it especially which assumes the state debts was pronounced unconstitutional. After the session of 1791 I again withdrew from the assembly, determined to bid a final adieu to political life.

The arrival and conduct of Mr. Genet excited great sensation throughout the southern states. We were all strongly attached to France—scarcely any man more strongly than myself. I sincerely believed human liberty to depend in a great measure on the success of the French revolution. My partiality to France however did not so entirely pervert my understanding as to render me insensible to the danger of permitting a foreign minister to mingle himself in the management of our affairs, and to intrude himself between our government and people. In a public meeting of the citizens of Richmond, some of the earliest if not the very first resolutions were passed expressing strong disapprobation of the irregular conduct of Mr. Genet, our decided sense of the danger of foreign influence, and our warm approbation of the proclamation of neutrality. These resolutions, and the address to the President which accompanied them, were drawn and supported by me.

The resentments of the great political party which led Virginia had been directed towards me for some time, but this measure brought it into active operation. I was attacked with great virulence in the papers and was so far honoured in Virginia as to be associated with Alexander Hamilton, at least so far as to be termed his instrument. With equal vivacity I defended myself and the measures of the government. My constant effort was to show that the conduct of our government respecting its foreign relations were such as a just self-respect and a regard for our rights as a sovereign nation rendered indispensable, and that our independence was brought into real danger by the overgrown & inordinate influence of France. . . .

In June 1797 I was placed by Mr. Adams, then President of the United States, in the commission for accomodating our differences with France, and received a letter requesting my attendance in Philadelphia in order to receive the communications of the government respecting the mission previous to my embarcation. It was the first time in my life that I had ever hesitated concerning the acceptance of office. My resolution concerning my profession had sustained no change. Indeed my circumstances required urgently that I should adhere to this resolution because I had engaged with some others in the purchase of a large estate the arrangements concerning which were not yet made. On the other hand I felt a very deep interest in the state of our controversy with France. I was most anxious and believed the government to be most anxious for the adjustment of our differences with that republic. I felt some confidence in the good dispositions which I should carry with me into the negotiation, and in the temperate firmness with which I should aid in the investigations which would be made. The subject was familiar to me, and had occupied a large portion of my thoughts. I will confess that the *eclat* which would attend a successful termination of the differences between the two countries had no small influence over a mind in which ambition, though subjected to controul, was not absolutely extinguished. But the consideration which decided me was this. The mission was temporary, and could not be of long duration. I should return after a short absence, to my profession, with no diminution of character, &, I trusted, with no diminution of practice. My clients would know immediately that I should soon return & I could make arrangements with the gentlemen of the bar which would prevent my business from suffering in the meantime. . . .

. . . A journal which I kept exhibits a curious account of transactions at Paris. As soon as I became perfectly convinced that our
efforts at conciliation must prove abortive I proposed that we should
address a memorial to Mr. Talleyrand in which we should review
fully the reciprocal complaints of the two countries against each
other, and bring the whole controversy, at least our view of it before
the French government in like manner as if we had been actually
accredited. My motive for this was that if the memorial should fail
to make its due impression on the government of France, it would
show the sincerity with which we had laboured to effect the objects
of our mission, and could not fail to bring the controversy fairly
before the American People and convince them of the earnestness
with which the American government sought a reconciliation with
France. General Pinckney concurred with me in sentiment and we
acted most cordially together. I found in him a sensible man, and
one of high and even romantic honour. Mr. Gerry took a different
view of the whole subject. He was unwilling to do anything, and it
was with infinite difficulty we prevailed on him to join us in the
letter to the minister of exterior relations. It was with the same
difficulty we prevailed on him to sign the reply to this answer of
the minister. We were impatient to hasten that reply from a fear
that we should be ordered to leave France before it could be sent.
We knew very well that this order would come and there was a
trial of skill between the minister and ourselves, (Genl. Pinckney &
myself) he endeavouring to force us to demand our passports, we
endeavouring to impose on him the necessity of sending them.
At length the passports came and I hastened to Bordeaux to em-
bark for the United States. On my arrival in New York I found
the whole country in a state of agitation on the subject of our mission. Our dispatches had been published and their effect on public
opinion had fully equalled my anticipations.

I returned to Richmond with a full determination to devote myself entirely to my professional duties, and was not a little delighted
to find that my prospects at the bar had sustained no material in-
jury from my absence. My friends welcomed my return with the
most flattering reception, and pressed me to become a candidate
for Congress. My refusal was peremptory, and I did not believe it
possible that my determination could be shaken. I was however
mistaken.

General Washington gave a pressing invitation to his nephew, the present Judge [Bushrod Washington], & myself, to pass a few days at Mount Vernon. He urged us both very earnestly to come into Congress & Mr. Washington assented to his wishes. I resisted, on the ground of my situation, & the necessity of attending to my pecuniary affairs. I can never forget the manner in which he treated this objection.

He said there were crises in national affairs which made it the duty of a citizen to forego his private for the public interest. We were then in one of them. He detailed his opinions freely on the nature of our controversy with France and expressed his conviction that the best interests of our country depended on the character of the ensuing Congress. He concluded a very earnest conversation, one of the most interesting I was ever engaged in, by asking my attention to his situation. He had retired from the Executive department with the firmest determination never again to appear in a public capacity. He had communicated this determination to the public, and his motives for adhering to it were too strong not to be well understood. Yet I saw him pledged to appear once more at the head of the American army. What must be his convictions of duty imposed by the present state of American affairs? . . .

My election was contested with unusual warmth, but I succeeded, and took my seat in the House of Representatives in Decr. 1799. There was a good deal of talent in that Congress both for and against the administration, and I contracted friendships with several gentlemen whom I shall never cease to value. The greater number of them are no more. . . .

. . . I had not been long in Virginia [in 1800] when the rupture between Mr. Adams and Mr. Pickering took place, and I was nominated to the senate as secretary of state. I never felt more doubt than on the question of accepting or declining this office. My decided preference was still for the bar. But on becoming a candidate for Congress I was given up as a lawyer, and considered generally as entirely a political man. I lost my business alltogether, and perceived very clearly that I could not recover any portion of it without retiring from Congress. Even then I could not hope to regain the ground I had lost. This experiment however I was willing to make, and would have made had my political enemies been quiet. But the press teemed with so much falsehood, with such continued and irritating abuse of me that I could not bring myself to yield to it. I could not conquer a stubbornness of temper which determines a man to make head against and struggle with injustice. I felt that I must continue a candidate for Congress, and consequently could not replace myself at the bar. On the other hand the office was precisely that which I wished, and for which I had vanity enough to think myself fitted. I should remain in it while the party remained in power; should a revolution take place it would at all events relieve me from the competition for Congress without yielding to my adversaries, and enable me to return once more to the bar in the character of a lawyer having no possible view to politics. I determined to accept the office. . . .

On the resignation of Chief Justice Ellsworth I recommended Judge Patteson [sic] as his successor. The President objected to him, and assigned as his ground of objection that the feelings of Judge Cushing would be wounded by passing him and selecting a junior member of the bench. I never heard him assign any other objection to Judge Patteson [sic], though it was afterwards suspected by many that he was believed to be connected with the party which opposed the second attempt at negotiation with France. The President himself mentioned Mr. Jay, and he was nominated to the senate. When I waited on the President with Mr. Jays letter declining the appointment he said thoughtfully "Who shall I nominate now"? I replied that I could not tell, as I supposed that his objection to Judge Patteson [sic] remained. He said in a decided tone "I shall not nominate him." After a moments hesitation he said "I believe I must nominate you." I had never before heard myself named for the office and had not even thought of it. I was pleased as well as surprized, and bowed in silence. Next day I was nominated, and, although the nomination was suspended by the friends of Judge Patteson [sic], it was I believe when taken up unanimously approved. I was unfeignedly gratified at the appointment, and have had much reason to be so. I soon received a very friendly letter from Judge Patteson [sic] congratulating me on the occasion and expressing [his] hopes that I might long retain the office. I felt truely grateful for the real cordiality towards me which uniformly marked his conduct.

2
Marshall and the Formation of the Constitution

Marshall's constitutional law doctrines evolved from his historical conception of the formation of the Constitution, as well as his political, social, and economic predilections. The idea that the United States, under the Articles of Confederation, suffered through a "critical period" when anarchy and economic chaos threatened the very existence of the young republic long dominated our historical understanding of the period. The national-minded Federalists promoted that notion as part of their campaign for a new constitution in the 1780s. As a participant in the Virginia ratifying convention in 1788, Marshall fully subscribed to these views and enthusiastically supported the Constitution of 1787. Nearly two decades later, he incorporated them into his multi-volumed account of the life and times of Washington. In later Supreme Court opinions, he regularly recalled the "discontents," the "disorderly spirits," and the ever-present threat of anarchy under the Articles, and he used that experience as justification for the exercise of governmental power under the new Constitution.

THE VIRGINIA CONVENTION: 1788 [1]

Marshall's remarks in the ratifying convention primarily covered the need for the Constitution and the expansion of national authority. It is, also, one of those marvelous accidents of history that the supporters of the Constitution selected him to discuss the proposed national judiciary and its powers.

[1] Jonathan Eliot, ed., *The Debate in the Several State Conventions on the Adoption of the Constitution* (Philadelphia, 1836–59), 5: 222–23, 226–32, 551–54.

The New Constitution

Permit me to attend to what the honorable gentleman (Mr. Henry) has said. He has expatiated on the necessity of a due attention to certain maxims—to certain fundamental principles, from which a free people ought never to depart. I concur with him in the propriety of the observance of such maxims. They are necessary in any government, but more essential to a democracy than to any other. What are the favorite maxims of democracy? A strict observance of justice and public faith, and a steady adherence to virtue. These, sir, are the principles of a good government. No mischief, no misfortune, ought to deter us from a strict observance of justice and public faith. Would to Heaven that these principles had been observed under the present government! Had this been the case, the friends of liberty would not be so willing now to part with it. Can we boast that our government is founded on these maxims? Can we pretend to the enjoyment of political freedom or security, when we are told that a man has been, by an act of Assembly, struck out of existence without a trial by jury, without examination, without being confronted with his accusers and witnesses, without the benefits of the law of the land? Where is our safety, when we are told that this act was justifiable because the person was not a Socrates? What has become of the worthy member's maxims? Is this one of them? Shall it be a maxim that a man shall be deprived of his life without the benefit of law? Shall such a deprivation of life be justified by answering, that the man's life was not taken *secundum artem* because he was a bad man? Shall it be a maxim that government ought not to be empowered to protect virtue? . . .

Let me pay attention to the observation of the gentleman who was last up, that the power of taxation ought not to be given to Congress. This subject requires the undivided attention of this house. This power I think essentially necessary; for without it there will be no efficiency in the government. We have had a sufficient demonstration of the vanity of depending on requisitions. How, then, can the general government exist without this power? The possibility of its being abused is urged as an argument against its expediency. To very little purpose did Virginia discover the defects in the old system; to little purpose, indeed, did she propose improvements; and to no purpose is this plan constructed for the promotion of our happiness, if we refuse it now, because it is possible that it may be abused. The Confederation has nominal powers, but no means to carry them into effect. If a system of government were devised by more than human intelligence, it would not be effectual if the means were not adequate to the power. All delegated powers are liable to be abused. Arguments drawn from this source go in direct opposition to the government, and in recommendation of anarchy. The friends of the Constitution are as tenacious of liberty as its enemies. They wish to give no power that will endanger it. They wish to give the government powers to secure and protect it. Our inquiry here must be, whether the power of taxation be necessary to perform the objects of the Constitution, and whether it be safe, and as well guarded as human wisdom can do it. What are the objects of the national government? To protect the United States, and to promote the general welfare. Protection, in time of war, is one of its principal objects. Until mankind shall cease to have ambition and avarice, wars will arise.

The prosperity and happiness of the people depend on the performance of these great and important duties of the general government. Can these duties be performed by one state? Can one state protect us, and promote our happiness? The honorable gentleman who has gone before me (Governor Randolph) has shown that Virginia cannot do these things. How, then, can they be done? By the national government only. Shall we refuse to give it power to do them? We are answered, that the powers may be abused; that, though the Congress may promote our happiness, yet they may prostitute their powers to destroy our liberties. This goes to the destruction of all confidence in agents. Would you believe that men who had merited your highest confidence would deceive you? Would you trust them again after one deception? Why then hesitate to trust the general government? The object of our inquiry is, *Is the power necessary, and is it guarded?* There must be men and money to protect us. How are armies to be raised? Must we not have money for that purpose? But the honorable gentleman says that we need not be afraid of war. Look at history, which has been so often quoted. Look at the great volume of human nature. They will foretell you that a defenceless country cannot be secure. The nature of man forbids us to conclude that we are in no danger from war. The passions of men stimulate them to avail themselves of the weakness of others. The powers of Europe are jealous of us. It is our interest to watch their conduct, and guard against them. They must be pleased with our disunion. If we invite them by our weakness to attack us, will they not do it? If we add debility to our present situation, a partition of America may take place.

It is, then, necessary to give the government that power, in time of peace, which the necessity of war will render indispensable, or else we shall be attacked unprepared. The experience of the world, a knowledge of human nature, and our own particular experience, will confirm this truth. When danger shall come upon us, may we not do what we were on the point of doing once already—that is, appoint a dictator? Were those who are now friends to this Constitution less active in the defence of liberty, on that trying occasion, than those who oppose it? When foreign dangers come, may not the fear of immediate destruction, by foreign enemies, impel us to take a most dangerous step? Where, then, will be our safety? We may now regulate and frame a plan that will enable us to repel attacks, and render a recurrence to dangerous expedients unnecessary. If we be prepared to defend ourselves, there will be little inducement to attack us. But if we defer giving the necessary power to the general government till the moment of danger arrives, we shall give it then, and with an *unsparing hand*. America, like other nations, may be exposed to war. The propriety of giving this power will be proved by the history of the world, and particularly of modern republics. I defy you to produce a single instance where requisitions on several individual states, composing a confederacy, have been honestly complied with. Did gentlemen expect to see such punctuality complied with in America? If they did, our own experience shows the contrary.

We are told that the Confederation carried us through the war. Had not the enthusiasm of liberty inspired us with unanimity, that system would never have carried us through it. It would have been much sooner terminated had that government been possessed of due energy. The inability of Congress, and the failure of states to comply with the constitutional requisitions, rendered our resistance less efficient than it might have been. The weakness of that government caused troops to be against us which ought to have been on our side, and prevented all resources of the community from being called at once into action. The extreme readiness of the people to make their utmost exertions to ward off solely the pressing danger, supplied the place of requisitions. When they came solely to be depended on, their inutility was fully discovered. A bare sense of duty, or a regard to propriety, is too feeble to induce men to comply with obligations. We deceive ourselves if we expect any efficacy from these. If requisitions will not avail, the government must have the sinews of war some other way. Requisitions cannot be effectual. They will be productive of delay, and will ultimately be inefficient. By direct taxation, the necessities of the government will be supplied in a peaceable manner, without irritating the minds of the people. But requisitions cannot be rendered efficient without a civil war—without great expense of money, and the blood of our citizens. Are there any other means? Yes, that Congress shall apportion the respective quotas previously, and if not complied with by the states, that then this dreaded power shall be exercised. The operation of this has been described by the gentleman who opened the debate. He cannot be answered. This great objection to that system remains unanswered. Is there no other argument which ought to have weight with us on this subject? Delay is a strong and pointed objection to it.

We are told by the gentleman who spoke last, that direct taxation is unnecessary, because we are not involved in war. This admits the propriety of recurring to direct taxation if we were engaged in war. It has not been proved that we have no dangers to apprehend on this point. What will be the consequence of the system proposed by the worthy gentleman? Suppose the states should refuse!

The worthy gentleman who is so pointedly opposed to the Constitution, proposes remonstrances. Is it a time for Congress to remonstrate, or compel a compliance with requisitions, when the whole wisdom of the Union, and the power of Congress, are opposed to a foreign enemy? Another alternative is, that, if the states shall appropriate certain funds for the use of Congress, Congress shall not lay direct taxes. Suppose the funds appropriated by the states for the use of Congress should be inadequate; it will not be determined whether they be insufficient till after the time at which the quota ought to have been paid; and then, after so long a delay, the means of procuring money, which ought to have been employed in the first instance, must be recurred to. May they not be amused by such ineffectual and temporizing alternatives from year to year, until America shall be enslaved? The failure in one state will authorize a failure in another. The calculation in some states that others will fail, will produce general failures. This will also be attended with all the expenses which we are anxious to avoid. What are the advantages to induce us to embrace this system? If they mean that requisitions should be complied with, it will be the same as if Congress had the power of direct taxation. The same amount will be paid by the people.

It is objected, that Congress will not know how to lay taxes so as to be easy and convenient for the people at large. Let us pay strict attention to this objection. If it appears to be totally without foundation, the necessity of levying direct taxes will obviate what the gentleman says; nor will there be any color for refusing to grant the power.

The objects of direct taxes are well understood: they are but few: what are they? Lands, slaves, stock of all kinds, and a few other articles of domestic property. Can you believe that ten men selected from all parts of the state, chosen because they know the situation of the people, will be unable to determine so as to make the tax equal on, and convenient for, the people at large? Does any man believe that they would lay the tax without the aid of other information besides their own knowledge, when they know that the very object for which they are elected is to lay the taxes in a judicious and convenient manner? If they wish to retain the affections of the people at large, will they not inform themselves of every circumstance that can throw light on the subject? Have they but one source of information? Besides their own experience—their knowledge of what will suit their constituents—they will have the benefit of the knowledge and experience of the state legislature. They will see in what manner the legislature of Virginia collects its taxes. Will they be unable to follow their example? The gentlemen who shall be delegated to Congress will have every source of information that the legislatures of the states can have, and can lay the taxes as equally on the people, and with as little oppression, as they can. If, then, it be admitted that they can understand how to lay them equally and conveniently, are we to admit that they will not do it, but that, in violation of every principle that ought to govern men, they will lay them so as to oppress us? What benefit will they have by it? Will it be promotive of their reëlection? Will it be by wantonly imposing hardships and difficulties on the people at large, that they will promote their own interest, and secure their reëlection? To me it appears incontrovertible that they will settle them in such a manner as to be easy for the people. Is the system so organized as to make taxation dangerous? I shall not go to the various checks of the government, but examine whether the immediate representation of the people be well constructed. I conceive its organization to be sufficiently satisfactory to the warmest friend of freedom. No tax can be laid without the consent of the House of Representatives. If there be no impropriety in the mode of electing the representatives, can any danger be apprehended? They are elected by those who can elect representatives in the state legislature. How can the votes of the electors be influenced? By nothing but the character and conduct of the man they vote for. What object can influence them when about choosing him? They have nothing to direct them in the choice but their own good. Have you not as pointed and strong a security as you can possibly have? It is a mode that secures an impossibility of being corrupted. If they are to be chosen for their wisdom, virtue, and integrity, what inducement have they to infringe on our freedom? We are told that they may abuse their power. Are there strong motives to prompt them to abuse it? Will not such abuse militate against their own interest? Will not they and their friends feel the effects of iniquitous measures? Does the representative remain in office for life? Does he transmit his title of representative to his son? Is he secured from the burden imposed on the community? To procure their reëlection, it will be necessary for them to confer with the people at large, and convince them that the taxes laid are for their good. If I am able to judge on the subject, the power of taxation now before us is wisely conceded, and the representatives are wisely elected.

The honorable gentleman said that a government should ever depend on the affections of the people. It must be so. It is the best support it can have. This government merits the confidence of the people, and, I make no doubt, will have it. Then he informed us again of the disposition of Spain with respect to the Mississippi, and the conduct of the government with regard to it. To the debility of the Confederation alone may justly be imputed every cause of complaint on this subject. Whenever gentlemen will bring forward their objections, I trust we can prove that no danger to the navigation of that river can arise from the adoption of this Constitution. I beg those gentlemen who may be affected by it, to suspend their judgment till they hear it discussed. Will, says he, the adoption of this Constitution pay our debts? It will compel the states to pay their quotas. Without this, Virginia will be unable to pay. Unless all the states pay, she cannot. Though the states will not coin money, (as we are told,) yet this government will bring forth and proportion all the strength of the Union. That economy and industry are essential to our happiness, will be denied by no man. But the present government will not add to our industry. It takes away the incitements to industry, by rendering property insecure and unprotected. It is the paper on your table that will promote and encourage industry. New Hampshire and Rhode Island have rejected it, he tells us. New Hampshire, if my information be right, will certainly adopt it. The report spread in this country, of which I have heard, is, that the representatives of that state having, on meeting, found they were instructed to vote against it, returned to their constituents without determining the question, to convince them of their being mistaken, and of the propriety of adopting it.

The extent of the country is urged as another objection, as being too great for a republican government. This objection has been handed from author to author, and has been certainly misunderstood and misapplied. To what does it owe its source? To observations and criticisms on governments, where representation did not exist. As to the legislative power, was it ever supposed inadequate to any extent? Extent of country may render it difficult to execute the laws, but not to legislate. Extent of country does not extend the power. What will be sufficiently energetic and operative in a small territory, will be feeble when extended over a wide-extended country. The gentleman tells us there are no checks in this plan. What has become of his enthusiastic eulogium on the American spirit? We should find a check and control, when oppressed, from that source. In this country, there is no exclusive personal stock of interest. The interest of the community is blended and inseparably connected with that of the individual. When he promotes his own, he promotes that of the community. When we consult the common good, we consult our own. When he desires such checks as these, he will find them abundantly here. They are the best checks. What has become of his eulogium on the Virginia Constitution? Do the checks in this plan appear less excellent than those of the Constitution of Virginia? If the checks in the Constitution be compared to the checks in the Virginia Constitution, he will find the best security in the former.

The temple of liberty was complete, said he, when the people of England said to their king, that he was their servant. What are we to learn from this? Shall we embrace such a system as that? Is not liberty secure with us, where the people hold all powers in their own hands, and delegate them cautiously, for short periods, to their servants, who are accountable for the smallest mal-administration? Where is the nation that can boast greater security than we do? We want only a system like the paper before you, to strengthen and perpetuate this security. . . .

The National Judiciary

Mr. Chairman, this part of the plan before us is a great improvement on that system from which we are now departing. Here are tribunals appointed for *the decision of controversies* which were before either not at all, or improperly, provided for. That many benefits will result from this to the members of the collective society, every one confesses. Unless its organization be defective, and so constructed as to injure, instead of accommodating, the convenience of the people, it merits our approbation. After such a candid and fair discussion by those gentlemen who support it,—after the very able manner in which they have investigated and examined it, —I conceived it would be no longer considered as so very defective, and that those who opposed it would be convinced of the impropriety of some of their objections. But I perceive they still continue the same opposition. Gentlemen have gone on an idea that the federal courts will not determine the causes which may come before them with the same fairness and impartiality with which other courts decide. What are the reasons of this supposition? Do they draw them from the manner in which the judges are chosen, or the tenure of their office? What is it that makes us trust our judges? Their independence in office, and manner of appointment. Are not the judges of the federal court chosen with as much wisdom as the judges of the state governments? Are they not equally, if not more independent? If so, shall we not conclude that they will decide with equal impartiality and candor? If there be as much wisdom and knowledge in the United States as in a particular state, shall we conclude that the wisdom and knowledge will not be equally exercised in the selection of judges?

The principle on which they object to the federal jurisdiction seems, to me, to be founded on a belief that there will not be a fair trial had in those courts. If this committee will consider it fully, they will find it has no foundation, and that we are as secure there as any where else. What mischief results from some causes being tried there? Is there not the utmost reason to conclude that judges, wisely appointed, and independent in their office, will never countenance any unfair trial? What are the subjects of its jurisdiction? Let us examine them with an expectation that causes will be as candidly tried there as elsewhere, and then determine. The objection which was made by the honorable member who was first up yesterday (Mr. Mason) has been so fully refuted that it is not worth while to notice it. He objected to Congress having power to create a number of inferior courts, according to the necessity of public circumstances. I had an apprehension that those gentlemen who placed no confidence in Congress would object that there might be no inferior courts. I own that I thought those gentlemen would think there would be no inferior courts, as it depended on the will of Congress, but that we should be dragged to the centre of the Union. But I did not conceive that the power of increasing the number of courts could be objected to by any gentleman, as it would remove the inconvenience of being dragged to the centre of the United States. I own that the power of creating a number of courts is, in my estimation, so far from being a defect, that it seems necessary to the perfection of this system. After having objected to the number and mode, he objected to the subject matter of their cognizance. [Here Mr. Marshall read the 2d section.]

These, sir, are the points of *federal jurisdiction* to which he objects, with a few exceptions. Let us examine each of them with a supposition that the same impartiality will be observed there as in other courts, and then see if any mischief will result from them. With respect to its cognizance in all cases arising under the Constitution and the laws of the United States, he says that, the laws of the United States being paramount to the laws of the particular states, there is no case but what this will extend to. Has the government of the United States power to make laws on every subject? Does he understand it so? Can they make laws affecting the mode of transferring property, or contracts, or claims, between citizens of the same state? Can they go beyond the delegated powers? If they were to make a law not warranted by any of the powers enumerated, it would be considered by the judges as an infringement of the Constitution which they are to guard. They would not consider such a law as coming under their jurisdiction. They would declare it void. It will annihilate the state courts, says the honorable gentleman. Does not every gentleman here know that the causes in our courts are more numerous than they can decide, according to their present construction? Look at the dockets. You will find them crowded with suits, which the life of man will not see determined. If some of these suits be carried to other courts, will it be wrong? They will still have business enough.

Then there is no danger that particular subjects, small in proportion, being taken out of the jurisdiction of the state judiciaries, will render them useless and of no effect. Does the gentleman think that the state courts will have no cognizance of cases not mentioned here? Are there any words in this Constitution which exclude the courts of the states from those cases which they now possess? Does the gentleman imagine this to be the case? Will any gentleman believe it? Are not controversies respecting lands claimed under the grants of different states the only controversies between citizens of the same state which the federal judiciary can take cognizance of? The case is so clear, that to prove it would be a useless waste of time. The state courts will not lose the jurisdiction of the causes they now decide. They have a concurrence of jurisdiction with the federal courts in those cases in which the latter have cognizance.

THE LIFE OF GEORGE WASHINGTON [2]

Marshall's historical effort often is overlooked as a source for understanding his judicial career. Admittedly, it is difficult reading—quite dry, terribly overwritten, and largely typical of the patriotic histories of the time. Yet it offers Marshall's most complete statement on American politics, the origins of the Constitution, and the partisanship of the 1790s. In this selection from his biography of Washington, Marshall describes conditions under the Articles of Confederation.

From peace, from independence, and from governments of her own choice, America had confidently anticipated every possible blessing. The glorious termination of their contest with one of the most powerful nations of the earth; the steady and persevering courage with which that contest had been maintained; and the unyielding firmness with which the privations attending it had been sup-

---

[2] John Marshall, *The Life of George Washington* . . . (Philadelphia, 1807), 5: 30–121, passim.

ported, had surrounded the infant republics with a great degree of splendor, and had bestowed upon them a character which could be preserved only by a national and dignified system of conduct. A very short time was sufficient to demonstrate, that something not yet possessed was requisite, to realize the public and private prosperity expected to flow from self government. After a short struggle so to administer the existing system as to make it competent to the great objects for which it was instituted, the effort became apparently desperate, and American affairs were impelled rapidly to a crisis, on which depended perhaps the continuance of the United States as a nation. . . .

In a government constituted like that of the United States, it would readily be expected that great contrariety of sentiment would prevail, respecting the principles on which the affairs of the union should be conducted. It has been already stated that the continent was divided into two great political parties, the one of which contemplated America as a nation, and laboured incessantly to invest the federal head with powers competent to the preservation of the union. The other attached itself to the state authorities, viewed all the powers of congress with jealousy; and assented reluctantly to measures which would enable the head to act, in any respect, independently of the members. Men of enlarged and liberal minds who, in the imbecility of a general government, by which alone the capacities of the nation could be efficaciously exerted, could discern the imbecility of the nation itself; who, viewing the situation of the world, could perceive the dangers to which these young republics were exposed, if not held together by a cement capable of preserving a beneficial connexion; who felt the full value of national honour, and the full obligation of national faith; and who were persuaded of the insecurity of both, if resting for their preservation on the concurrence of thirteen distinct sovereignties; arranged themselves generally in the first party. The officers of the army, whose local prejudices had been weakened by associating with each other, and whose experience had furnished lessons on the inefficacy of requisitions which were not soon to be forgotten, threw their weight almost universally into the same scale.

As if sensible that the character of the government would be decided in a considerable degree by the measures which should immediately follow the treaty of peace, gentlemen of the first political abilities and integrity, among whom were some who, after performing a distinguished part in the military transactions of the continent, had retired from the army, sought a place in the congress of 1783. Combining their efforts for the establishment of principles on which the honour and the interest of the nation were believed to depend, they exerted all their talents to impress on the several states, the necessity of conferring on the government of the union, powers which might be competent to its preservation, and which would enable it to comply with the engagements it had formed. With unwearied perseverance they digested and obtained the assent of congress to a system, which, though unequal to what their wishes would have prepared, or their judgments have approved, was believed to be the best that was attainable. The great object in view was, "to restore and support public credit," to effect which it was necessary, "to obtain from the states substantial funds for funding the whole debt of the United States."

The committee to whom this interesting subject was referred, was composed of persons alike distinguished for their intelligence, for their attachment to the union, and for their veneration of the public faith. They reported sundry resolutions, recommending it to the several states, to vest in congress permanent and productive funds adequate to the immediate payment of the interest on the national debt, and to the gradual extinction of the principal. These funds were to be raised in part by duties on imported articles; and in part by internal taxes. A change in the rule by which the proportions of the different states were to be ascertained was also recommended. In lieu of that article of the confederation which apportions on them the sums required for the public treasury, according to the value of their located lands with the improvements thereon, it was proposed to substitute another more capable of execution, which should make the population of each state the measure of its contribution.

It was readily perceived, that if the provision made by the states should prove inadequate to the claims of all the public creditors, its distribution would be partial; and that the less favoured, who might be neglected, would be reduced to a still more hopeless condition by being separated from the great mass whose demands it was thought impossible to disregard. To obviate this manifest injustice, it was declared that no part of the revenue system should take effect until the whole should be acceded to by all the states; after which, every part of the grant was to be irrevocable, except by the concurrence of the whole, or of a majority of the United States in congress assembled. . . .

The recommendations of congress did not receive that prompt consideration which the public exigence demanded, nor did they meet that universal assent which was necessary to give them effect.

Not immediately perceiving that the error lay in a system which was absolutely unfit for use, the distinguished patriots of the revolution contemplated with infinite anxiety, the anti-American temper which displayed itself in almost every part of the union. . . .

That the imbecility of the federal government, the impotence of its requisitions, and the inattention of some of the states to its recommendations, would in the estimation of the world, abase the American character, could scarcely be termed a prediction. From its inability to protect the general interests, or to comply with its political or pecuniary engagements, already had that course of national degradation commenced which such a state of things must necessarily produce.

As the system recommended to the states on the 18th of April 1783, had been matured by the best wisdom in the federal councils, a compliance with it was the last hope of the government; and congress continued to urge its adoption on the several states. While its fate remained undecided, requisitions for the intermediate supply of the national demands were annually repeated, and were annually neglected. . . .

To the enlightened and virtuous statesmen with whom that measure originated, it appeared impossible that their countrymen would be so unmindful of the obligations of honour and of justice, or could so misjudge their real interests, as to withhold their assent from the entire plan, if convinced that no partial compliance with it would be received. . . .

While the friends of the national government were making these unavailing efforts to invest it with a revenue which might enable it to preserve the national faith, many other causes concurred to prepare the public mind for some great and radical change in the political system of America. . . .

The discontents and uneasiness, arising in a great measure from the embarrassments in which a considerable number of individuals were involved, continued to become more extensive. At length, two great parties were formed in every state, which were distinctly marked, and which pursued distinct objects, with systematic arrangement.

The one struggled with unabated zeal for the exact observance of public and private engagements. By those belonging to it, the faith of a nation, or of a private man was deemed a sacred pledge, the violation of which was equally forbidden by the principles of moral justice, and of sound policy. The distresses of individuals were, they thought, to be alleviated only by industry and frugality, not by a relaxation of the laws, or by a sacrifice of the rights of others. According to the stern principles laid down for their government, the imprudent and idle could not be protected by the legislature from the consequences of their indiscretion; but should be restrained from involving themselves in difficulties, by the conviction that a rigid compliance with contracts would be enforced. They were consequently the uniform friends of a regular administration of justice, and of a vigorous course of taxation which would enable the state to comply with its engagements. By a natural association of ideas, they were also, with very few exceptions, in favour of enlarging the powers of the federal government, and of enabling it to protect the dignity and character of the nation abroad, and its interests at home. The other party marked out for itself a more indulgent course. Viewing with extreme tenderness the case of the debtor, their efforts were unceasingly directed to his relief. To exact a faithful compliance with contracts was, in their opinion, a measure too harsh to be insisted on, and was one which the people would not bear. They were uniformly in favour of relaxing the administration of justice, of affording facilities for the payment of debts, or of suspending their collection, and of remitting taxes. The same course of opinion led them to resist every attempt to transfer from their own hands into those of congress, powers which by others were deemed essential to the preservation of the union. In many of the states, the party last mentioned constituted a decided majority of the people; and in all of them, it was very powerful. The emission of paper money, the delay of legal proceedings, and the suspension of the collection of taxes, were the fruits of their rule wherever they were completely dominant. Even where they failed in carrying their measures, their strength was such as to encourage the hope of succeeding in a future attempt; and annual elections held forth to them the prospect of speedily repairing the loss of a favourite question. Throughout the union, the contest between these parties was periodically revived; and the public mind was perpetually agitated with hopes and fears on subjects which essentially affected the fortunes of a considerable proportion of the society.

These contests were the more animated, because, in the state governments generally, no principle had been introduced which could resist the wild projects of the moment, give the people an opportunity to reflect, and allow the good sense of the nation time for exertion. This uncertainty with respect to measures of great importance to every member of the community, this instability in principles which ought if possible to be rendered immutable, produced a long train of ills; and is seriously believed to have been among the operating causes of those pecuniary embarrassments, which at that time were so general as to influence the legislation of almost every state in the union. Its direct consequence was the loss of confidence in the government, and in individuals. This, so far as respected the government, was peculiarly discernible in the value of state debts. . . .

The hope and fear still remained, that the debtor party would obtain the victory at the elections; and instead of making the painful effort to obtain relief by industry and economy, many rested all their hopes on legislative interference. The mass of national labour, and of national wealth, was consequently diminished. In every quarter were found those who asserted it to be impossible for the people to pay their public or private debts; and in some instances, threats were uttered of suspending the administration of justice by private violence.

By the enlightened friends of republican government, this gloomy state of things was viewed with infinite chagrin; and many became apprehensive that those plans from which so much happiness to the human race had been anticipated, would produce only real misery; and would maintain but a short and a turbulent existence. Meanwhile, the wise and thinking part of the community, who could trace evils to their source, laboured unceasingly to inculcate opinions favourable to the incorporation of some principles into the political system, which might correct the obvious vices, without endangering the free spirit of the existing institutions. . . .

By the enlightened friends of the union and of republican government, the [constitutional] convention was generally regarded as a measure which afforded the best chance for preserving liberty and internal peace. . . .

There were many who had sketched in their own minds a plan of government strongly resembling that which has been actually adopted, but who despaired of seeing so rational a system accepted, or even recommended. . . .

There were many who discountenanced the convention, because the mode of calling it was deemed irregular, and some objected to it, because it was not so constituted as to give authority to the plan which should be devised. But the great mass of opposition originated in a devotion to state sovereignty, and in hostility to any considerable augmentation of federal authority.

The ultimate decision of the states on this interesting proposition seems to have been in some degree influenced by the commotions which about that time agitated all New England, and particularly Massachusetts.

Those causes of discontent which have been stated to have existed after the restoration of peace, in every part of the union, were no where more operative than in New England. The great exertions which had been made by those states in the course of the war, had accumulated a mass of debt, the taxes for the payment of which were the more burdensome, because their fisheries had become unproductive. This important branch of industry, which, before the revolution, had in some measure compensated for the want of those rich staples that were possessed by the middle and southern colonies, had been unavoidably neglected during the struggle for independence: and, as a consequence of that independence, had not only been deprived of the encouragements under which it had flourished, but its produce was excluded from markets which had formerly been open to it. The restlessness produced by the uneasy situation of individuals, connected with lax notions concerning public and private faith, and erroneous opinions which confound liberty with an exemption from legal control, produced a state of things which alarmed all reflecting men, and demonstrated to many the indispensable necessity of clothing government with powers sufficiently ample for the protection of the rights of the peaceable and quiet, from the invasions of the licentious and turbulent part of the community.

This disorderly spirit was cherished by unlicensed conventions, which, after voting their own constitutionality, and assuming the name of the people, arrayed themselves against the legislature, and detailed at great length the grievances by which they alleged themselves to be oppressed. Its hostility was principally directed against the compensation promised to the officers of the army, against taxes, and against the administration of justice: and the circulation of a depreciated currency was required, as a relief from the pressure of public and private burdens which had become, it was alleged, too heavy to be borne. Against lawyers and courts, the strongest resentments were manifested; and to such a dangerous extent were these dispositions indulged, that, in many instances, tumultuous assemblages of people arrested the course of law, and restrained the judges from proceeding in the execution of their duty. The ordinary recourse to the power of the county was found an insufficient security, and the appeals made to reason were attended with no beneficial effect. The forbearance of the government was attributed to timidity rather than to moderation, and the spirit of insurrection appeared to be organized into a regular system for the suppression of courts.

In the bosom of Washington, these tumults excited attention and alarm. "For God's sake tell me," said he in a letter to colonel Humphries, "what is the cause of all these commotions? do they proceed from licentiousness, British influence disseminated by the tories, or real grievances which admit of redress? if the latter, why was redress delayed until the public mind had become so much agitated? if the former, why are not the powers of government tried at once? it is as well to be without, as not to exercise them. Commotions of this sort, like snow balls, gather strength as they roll, if there is no opposition in the way to divide and crumble them." . . .

Finding that the lenient measures which had been taken by the legislature to subdue the resentments of the insurgents only enlarged their demands; that the pardon proffered to those who would return to their duty was rejected with scorn; that the conciliating efforts of government only increased their audacity; and that they were proceeding systematically to organize a military force for the subversion of the constitution; governor Bowdoin, who had been probably restrained by the temper manifested by the house of representatives from an earlier resort to force, at length determined, with the advice of council, on a vigorous exertion of all the powers he possessed, for the protection and defence of the commonwealth.

Upwards of four thousand militia were ordered into service, and were placed under the command of the veteran general Lincoln. . . .

At length, with the loss of a few killed and several prisoners, the rebels were dispersed, their leaders driven out of the state, and this formidable and wicked rebellion was completely quelled.

The same love of country which had supported the officers and soldiers of the late army through a perilous war, still glowed in their bosoms; and the patriot veterans of the revolution, uninfected by the wide spreading contagion of the times, arrayed themselves almost universally under the banners of the constitution and of the laws. This circumstance lessened the prejudices which had been excited against them as creditors of the public, and diminished the odium which, in the eastern states especially, had been directed against the order of the cincinnati. But the most important effect of this unprovoked rebellion was, the deep conviction it produced of the necessity of enlarging the powers of the general government, and the consequent direction of the public mind towards the convention which was to assemble at Philadelphia. . . .

At the time and place appointed, the representatives of twelve states convened. In Rhode Island alone was found a spirit sufficiently hostile to every species of reform, to prevent the election of deputies on an occasion so generally deemed momentous. Having unanimously chosen general Washington for their president, the convention proceeded, with closed doors, to discuss the interesting and extensive subject submitted to their consideration.

On the great principles which should constitute the basis of their system, not much contrariety of opinion is understood to have prevailed. But on the various and intricate modifications of those principles, an equal degree of harmony was not to be expected. More than once, there was reason to fear that the rich harvest of national felicity which had been anticipated from the ample stock of worth collected in convention, would all be blasted by the rising of that body without effecting the object for which it was formed. At length, the high importance which was attached to union triumphed over local interests; and on the 17th of September, that constitution which has been alike the theme of panegyric and invective, was presented to the American world.

3

Chief Justice Marshall and the Constitution

FEDERAL JUDICIAL POWER

Marbury v. Madison[1]

Marbury v. Madison provided Marshall with the opportunity for asserting a judicial veto over acts of Congress. Though not specifically enumerated in the Constitution, many contemporaries believed that the power existed as an assumed corollary to the idea of a written, supreme constitution and as part of the judicial function. Political and partisan considerations figured prominently in the case. In his last weeks as president, John Adams appointed numerous new justices of the peace for the District of Columbia. One, William Marbury, had been duly nominated and confirmed, but outgoing Secretary of State John Marshall failed to deliver his commission. When James Madison, Marshall's successor, refused to do so, Marbury sought a writ of mandamus directing the secretary to present the commission. In a tactical masterpiece, Marshall deftly sacrificed Marbury's cause for his own, higher aim of invoking judicial review—and all to the consternation and frustration of some of his Jeffersonian enemies.

In the order in which the court has viewed this subject, the following questions have been considered and decided: 1st. Has the applicant a right to the commission he demands? 2d. If he has a right, and that right has been violated, do the laws of his country afford him a remedy? 3d. If they do afford him a remedy, is it a *mandamus* issuing from this court? . . .

It is . . . the opinion of the Court: 1st. That by signing the commission of Mr. Marbury, the President of the United States appointed him a justice of peace for the county of Washington, in the

[1] 1 Cranch 137 (1803).

district of Columbia; and that the seal of the United States, affixed thereto by the secretary of state, is conclusive testimony of the verity of the signature, and of the completion of the appointment; and that the appointment conferred on him a legal right to the office for the space of five years. 2d. That, having this legal title to the office, he has a consequent right to the commission; a refusal to deliver which is a plain violation of that right, for which the laws of his country afford him a remedy.

3. It remains to be inquired whether he is entitled to the remedy for which he applies? This depends on—1st. The nature of the writ applied for; and 2d. The power of this court. . . .

This . . . is a plain case for a *mandamus,* either to deliver the commission, or a copy of it from the record; and it only remains to be inquired, whether it can issue from this court?

The act to establish the judicial courts of the United States authorizes the supreme court, "to issue writs of *mandamus,* in cases warranted by the principles and usages of law, to any courts appointed or persons holding office, under the authority of the United States." [Judiciary Act of 1789, Section 13.]. The secretary of state, being a person holding an office under the authority of the United States, is precisely within the letter of this description; and if this court is not authorized to issue a writ of *mandamus* to such an officer, it must be because the law is unconstitutional, and therefore, absolutely incapable of conferring the authority, and assigning the duties which its words purport to confer and assign.

The constitution vests the whole judicial power of the United States in one supreme court, and such inferior courts as congress shall, from time to time, ordain and establish. This power is expressly extended to all cases arising under the laws of the United States; and consequently, in some form, may be exercised over the present case; because the right claimed is given by a law of the United States.

In the distribution of this power, it is declared, that "the supreme court shall have original jurisdiction, in all cases affecting ambassadors, other public ministers and consuls, and those in which a state shall be a party. In all other cases, the supreme court shall have appellate jurisdiction." It has been insisted, at the bar, that as the original grant of jurisdiction to the supreme and inferior courts, is general, and the clause, assigning original jurisdiction to the supreme court, contains no negative or restrictive words, the power remains to the legislature, to assign original jurisdiction to that court, in other cases than those specified in the article which has been recited; provided those cases belong to the judicial power of the United States.

If it had been intended to leave it in the discretion of the legislature, to apportion the judicial power between the supreme and inferior courts, according to the will of that body, it would certainly have been useless to have proceeded further than to have defined the judicial power, and the tribunals in which it should be vested. The subsequent part of the section is mere surplusage—is entirely without meaning, if such is to be the construction. If congress remains at liberty to give this court appellate jurisdiction, where the constitution has declared their jurisdiction shall be original; and original jurisdiction where the constitution has declared it shall be appellate; the distribution of jurisdiction, made in the constitution, is form without substance. . . .

It has been stated at the bar, that the appellate jurisdiction may be exercised in a variety of forms, and that if it be the will of the legislature that a *mandamus* should be used for that purpose, that will must be obeyed. This is true, yet the jurisdiction must be appellate, not original. It is the essential criterion of appellate jurisdiction, that it revises and corrects the proceedings in a cause already instituted, and does not create that cause. Although, therefore, a *mandamus* may be directed to courts, yet to issue such a writ to an officer, for the delivery of a paper, is, in effect, the same as to sustain an original action for that paper, and therefore, seems not to belong to appellate, but to original jurisdiction. Neither is it necessary in such a case as this, to enable the court to exercise its appellate jurisdiction. The authority, therefore, given to the supreme court by the act establishing the judicial courts of the United States, to issue writs of *mandamus* to public officers, appears not to be warranted by the constitution; and it becomes necessary to inquire, whether a jurisdiction so conferred can be exercised.

The question, whether an act, repugnant to the constitution, can become the law of the land, is a question deeply interesting to the United States; but, happily, not of an intricacy proportioned to its interest. It seems only necessary to recognise certain principles, supposed to have been long and well established, to decide it. That the people have an original right to establish, for their future government, such principles as, in their opinion, shall most conduce to their own happiness, is the basis on which the whole American fabric has been erected. The exercise of this original right is a very great exertion; nor can it, nor ought it, to be frequently repeated. The principles, therefore, so established, are deemed fundamental: and as the authority from which they proceed is supreme, and can seldom act, they are designed to be permanent.

This original and supreme will organizes the government, and assigns to different departments their respective powers. It may either stop here, or establish certain limits not to be transcended by those departments. The government of the United States is of the latter description. The powers of the legislature are defined and limited; and that those limits may not be mistaken or forgotten, the constitution is written. To what purpose are powers limited, and to what purpose is that limitation committed to writing, if these limits may, at any time, be passed by those intended to be restrained? The distinction between a government with limited and unlimited powers is abolished, if those limits do not confine the persons on whom they are imposed, and if acts prohibited and acts allowed, are of equal obligation. It is a proposition too plain to be contested, that the constitution controls any legislative act repugnant to it; or that the legislature may alter the constitution by an ordinary act.

Between these alternatives, there is no middle ground. The constitution is either a superior paramount law, unchangeable by ordinary means, or it is on a level with ordinary legislative acts, and, like other acts, is alterable when the legislature shall please to alter it. If the former part of the alternative be true, then a legislative act, contrary to the constitution, is not law: if the latter part be true, then written constitutions are absurd attempts, on the part of the people, to limit a power, in its own nature, illimitable.

Certainly, all those who have framed written constitutions contemplate them as forming the fundamental and paramount law of the nation, and consequently, the theory of every such government must be, that an act of the legislature, repugnant to the constitution, is void. This theory is essentially attached to a written constitution, and is, consequently, to be considered, by this court, as one of the fundamental principles of our society. It is not, therefore, to be lost sight of, in the further consideration of this subject. . . .

It is, emphatically, the province and duty of the judicial department, to say what the law is. Those who apply the rule to particular cases, must of necessity expound and interpret that rule. If two laws conflict with each other, the courts must decide on the operation of each. So, if a law be in opposition to the constitution; if both the law and the constitution apply to a particular case, so that the court must either decide that case, conformable to the law, disregarding the constitution; or conformable to the constitution, disregarding the law; the court must determine which of these conflicting rules governs the case: this is of the very essence of judicial duty. If then, the courts are to regard the constitution, and the constitution is superior to any ordinary act of the legislature, the constitution, and not such ordinary act, must govern the case to which they both apply.

Those, then, who controvert the principle, that the constitution is to be considered, in court, as a paramount law, are reduced to the necessity of maintaining that courts must close their eyes on the constitution, and see only the law. This doctrine would subvert the very foundation of all written constitutions. It would declare that an act which, according to the principles and theory of our government, is entirely void, is yet, in practice, completely obligatory. It would declare, that if the legislature shall do what is expressly forbidden, such act, notwithstanding the express prohibition, is in reality effectual. It would be giving to the legislature a practical and real omnipotence, with the same breath which professes to restrict their powers within narrow limits. It is prescribing limits, and declaring that those limits may be passed at pleasure. That it thus reduces to nothing, what we have deemed the greatest improvement on political institutions, a written constitution, would, of itself, be sufficient, in America, where written constitutions have been viewed with so much reverence, for rejecting the construction. But the peculiar expressions of the constitution of the United States furnish additional arguments in favor of its rejection. The judicial power of the United States is extended to all cases arising under the constitution. Could it be the intention of those who gave this power, to say, that in using it, the constitution should not be looked into? That a case arising under the constitution should be decided, without examining the instrument under which it arises? This is too extravagant to be maintained. In some cases, then, the constitution must be looked into by the judges. And if they can open it at all, what part of it are they forbidden to read or to obey? . . .

[It] is apparent, that the framers of the constitution contemplated that instrument as a rule for the government of courts, as well as of the legislature. Why otherwise does it direct the judges to take an oath to support it? This oath certainly applies in an especial manner, to their conduct in their official character. How immoral to impose it on them, if they were to be used as the instruments, and the knowing instruments, for violating what they swear to support!

The oath of office, too, imposed by the legislature, is completely demonstrative of the legislative opinion on this subject. . . . Why does a judge swear to discharge his duties agreeably to the constitution of the United States, if that constitution forms no rule for his government? if it is closed upon him, and cannot be inspected by him? If such be the real state of things, this is worse than solemn mockery. To prescribe, or to take this oath, becomes equally a crime.

It is also not entirely unworthy of observation, that in declaring what shall be the supreme law of the land, the constitution itself is first mentioned; and not the laws of the United States, generally, but those only which shall be made in pursuance of the constitution, have that rank.

Thus, the particular phraseology of the constitution of the United States confirms and strengthens the principle, supposed to be essential to all written constitutions, that a law repugnant to the constitution is void; and that courts, as well as other departments, are bound by that instrument.

The rule must be discharged.

Cohens v. Virginia[2]

Section 25 of the Judiciary Act of 1789 authorized the Supreme Court to take appeals from state courts under certain conditions. Because of national-state power differences in the early nineteenth century, the scope of the Court's appellate jurisdiction aroused more controversy than judicial review of congressional laws. The Cohens had been arrested and convicted in Virginia for selling lottery tickets in violation of state law. As Congress had authorized the lottery for the benefit of the District of Columbia, the defendants appealed to the federal court over the bitter protest of Virginia courts and officials. Marshall sustained the Cohens' conviction but emphatically rejected Virginia's claim that its courts' judgments were

[2] 6 Wheaton 264 (1821).

*final in matters involving state laws. Despite an outpouring of
"states'-rights" rhetoric and various attempts (until the Civil
War) to repeal Section 25, Marshall's decision survived and
persists today as the basic precedent for federal judicial supremacy.*

The first question to be considered is, whether the jurisdiction
of this court is excluded by the character of the parties, one of them
being a State, and the other a citizen of that State?

The 2d section of the third article of the constitution defines the
extent of the judicial power of the United States. Jurisdiction is
given to the courts of the Union in two classes of cases. In the first,
their jurisdiction depends on the character of the cause, whoever
may be the parties. This class comprehends "all cases in law and
equity arising under this constitution, the laws of the United States,
and treaties made, or which shall be made, under their authority."
This clause extends the jurisdiction of the court to all the cases
described, without making in its terms any exception whatever, and
without any regard to the condition of the party. If there be any
exception, it is to be implied against the express words of the
article.

In the second class, the jurisdiction depends entirely on the character of the parties. In this are comprehended "controversies between two or more States, between a State and citizens of another
State," "and between a State and foreign states, citizens, or subjects." If these be the parties, it is entirely unimportant what may
be the subject of controversy. Be it what it may, these parties have
a constitutional right to come into the courts of the Union. . . .

The jurisdiction of the court, then, being extended by the letter
of the constitution to all cases arising under it, or under the laws
of the *United* States, it follows that those would withdraw any case
of this description from that jurisdiction, must sustain the exemption they claim on the spirit and true meaning of the constitution,
which spirit and true meaning must be so apparent as to overrule
the words which its framers have employed.

The counsel for the defendant in error have undertaken to do
this; and have laid down the general proposition, that a sovereign
independent State is not suable, except by its own consent.

This general proposition will not be controverted. But its consent is not requisite in each particular case. . . .

The American States, as well as the American people, have believed a close and firm Union to be essential to their liberty and to their happiness. They have been taught by experience, that this Union cannot exist without a government for the whole; and they have been taught by the same experience that this government would be a mere shadow, that must disappoint all their hopes, unless invested with large portions of that sovereignty which belongs to independent States. Under the influence of this opinion, and thus instructed by experience, the American people, in the conventions of their respective States, adopted the present constitution.

If it could be doubted whether, from its nature, it were not supreme in all cases where it is empowered to act, that doubt would be removed by the declaration that "this constitution, and the laws of the United States which shall be made in pursuance thereof, and all treaties made, or which shall be made, under the authority of the United States, shall be the supreme law of the land; and the judges in every State shall be bound thereby, any thing in the constitution or laws of any State to the contrary notwithstanding."

This is the authoritative language of the American people; and, if gentlemen please, of the American States. It marks with lines too strong to be mistaken, the characteristic distinction between the government of the Union and those of the States. The general government, though limited as to its objects, is supreme with respect to those objects. This principle is a part of the constitution; and if there be any who deny its necessity, none can deny its authority. . . .

With the ample powers confided to this supreme government, for these interesting purposes, are connected many express and important limitations on the sovereignty of the States, which are made for the same purposes. The powers of the Union, on the great subjects of war, peace, and commerce, and on many others, are in themselves limitations of the sovereignty of the States; but in addition to these, the sovereignty of the States is surrendered in many instances where the surrender can only operate to the benefit of the people, and where, perhaps, no other power is conferred on congress than a conservative power to maintain the principles established in the constitution. The maintenance of these principles in their purity, is certainly among the great duties of the government. One of the instruments by which this duty may be peaceably performed, is the judicial department. . . .

One of the express objects, then, for which the judicial department was established, is the decision of controversies between States, and between a State and individuals. The mere circumstance that a State is a party, gives jurisdiction to the court. How, then, can it be contended, that the very same instrument, in the very same section, should be so construed, as that this same circumstance should withdraw a case from the jurisdiction of the court, where the constitution or laws of the United States are supposed to have been violated? The constitution gave to every person having a claim upon a State, a right to submit his case to the court of the nation. However unimportant his claim might be, however little the community might be interested in its decision, the framers of our constitution thought it necessary for the purposes of justice, to provide a tribunal as superior to influence as possible, in which that claim might be decided. Can it be imagined, that the same persons considered a case involving the constitution of our country and the majesty of the laws, questions in which every American citizen must be deeply interested, as withdrawn from this tribunal, because a State is a party? . . .

But a constitution is framed for ages to come, and is designed to approach immortality as nearly as human institutions can approach it. Its course cannot always be tranquil. It is exposed to storms and tempests, and its framers must be unwise statesmen, indeed, if they have not provided it, as far as its nature will permit, with the means of self-preservation from the perils it may be destined to encounter. No government ought to be so defective in its organization, as not to contain within itself the means of securing the execution of its own laws against other dangers than those which occur every day. Courts of justice are the means most usually employed; and it is reasonable to expect that a government should repose on its own courts, rather than on others. There is certainly nothing in the circumstances under which our constitution was formed; nothing in the history of the times, which would justify the opinion that the confidence reposed in the States was so implicit as to leave in them and their tribunals the power of resisting or defeating, in the form of law, the legitimate measures of the Union. The requisitions of congress, under the confederation, were as constitutionally obligatory as the laws enacted by the present congress. That they were habitually disregarded, is a fact of universal notoriety. With the knowledge of this fact, and under its full pressure, a convention was assembled to change the system. Is it so improbable that they should confer on the judicial department the power of construing the constitution and laws of the Union in every case, in the last resort, and of preserving them from all violation from every quarter, so far as judicial decisions can preserve them, that this improbability should essentially affect the construction of the new system? We are told, and we are truly told, that the great change which is to give efficacy to the present system, is its ability to act on individuals directly, instead of acting through the instrumentality of state governments. But, ought not this ability, in reason and sound policy, to be applied directly to the protection of individuals employed in the execution of the laws, as well as to their coercion? Your laws reach the individual without the aid of any other power; why may they not protect him from punishment for performing his duty in executing them? . . .

It is very true that, whenever hostility to the existing system shall become universal, it will be also irresistible. The people made the constitution, and the people can unmake it. It is the creature of their will, and lives only by their will. But this supreme and irresistible power to make or to unmake resides only in the whole body of the people; not in any subdivision of them. The attempt of any of the parts to exercise it is usurpation, and ought to be repelled by those to whom the people have delegated their power of repelling it. . . .

The constitution declares that in cases where a State is a party, the supreme court shall have original jurisdiction; but does not say that its appellate jurisdiction shall not be exercised in cases where, from their nature, appellate jurisdiction is given, whether a State be or be not a party. It may be conceded, that where the case is of such a nature as to admit of its originating in the supreme court, it ought to originate there; but where, from its nature, it cannot originate in that court, these words ought not to be so construed as to require it. There are many cases in which it would be found extremely difficult, and subversive of the spirit of the constitution, to maintain the construction that appellate jurisdiction cannot be exercised where one of the parties might sue or be sued in this court. . . .

It is most true that this court will not take jurisdiction if it should not; but it is equally true, that it must take jurisdicion if it should. The judiciary cannot, as the legislature may, avoid a measure because it approaches the confines of the constitution. We cannot pass it by because it is doubtful. With whatever doubts, with whatever difficulties, a case may be attended, we must decide it, if it be brought before us. We have no more right to decline the exercise of jurisdiction which is given, than to usurp that which is not given. The one or the other would be treason to the constitution. Questions may occur which we would gladly avoid; but we cannot avoid them. All we can do is, to exercise our best judgment, and conscientiously to perform our duty. In doing this on the present occasion, we find this tribunal invested with appellate jurisdiction in all cases arising under the constitution and laws of the United States. We find no exception to this grant, and we cannot insert one. . . .

It is, then, the opinion of the court, that the defendant who removes a judgment rendered against him by a state court into this court, for the purpose of reëxamining the question whether that judgment be in violation of the constitution or laws of the United States, does not commence or prosecute a suit against the State, whatever may be its opinion where the effect of the writ may be to restore the party to the possession of a thing which he demands. . . .

The second objection to the jurisdiction of the court is, that its appellate power cannot be exercised, in any case, over the judgment of a state court.

This objection is sustained chiefly by arguments drawn from the supposed total separation of the judiciary of a State from that of the Union, and their entire independence of each other. The argument considers the federal judiciary as completely foreign to that of a State; and as being no more connected with it, in any respect whatever, than the court of a foreign state. If this hypothesis be just, the argument founded on it is equally so; but if the hypothesis be not supported by the constitution, the argument fails with it. . . .

That the United States form, for many, and for most important purposes, a single nation, has not yet been denied. In war, we are one people. In making peace, we are one people. In all commercial regulations, we are one and the same people. In many other respects, the American people are one; and the government which is alone capable of controlling and managing their interests, in all these respects, is the government of the Union. It is their government, and in that character they have no other. America has chosen to be, in many respects, and to many purposes, a nation; and for all these purposes her government is complete; to all these objects, it is competent. The people have declared, that in the exercise of all powers given for these objects, it is supreme. It can, then, in effecting these objects, legitimately control all individuals or governments within the American territory. The constitution and laws of a State, so far as they are repugnant to the constitution and laws of the United States, are absolutely void. These States are constituent parts of the United States. They are members of one great empire—for some purposes sovereign, for some purposes subordinate.

In a government so constituted, is it unreasonable that the judicial power should be competent to give efficacy to the constitutional laws of the legislature? That department can decide on the validity of the constitution or law of a State, if it be repugnant to the constitution or to a law of the United States. Is it unreasonable that it should also be empowered to decide on the judgment of a state tribunal enforcing such unconstitutional law? Is it so very unreasonable as to furnish a justification for controlling the words of the constitution?

We think it is not. We think that in a government acknowledgedly supreme, with respect to objects of vital interest to the nation, there is nothing inconsistent with sound reason, nothing incompatible with the nature of government, in making all its departments supreme, so far as respects those objects, and so far as is necessary to their attainment. The exercise of the appellate power over those judgments of the state tribunals which may contravene the constitution or laws of the United States, is, we believe, essential to the attainment of those objects.

The propriety of intrusting the construction of the constitution, and laws made in pursuance thereof, to the judiciary of the Union, has not, we believe, as yet, been drawn into question. It seems to be a corollary from this political axiom, that the federal courts should either possess exclusive jurisdiction in such cases, or a power to revise the judgment rendered in them by the state tribunals. If the federal and state courts have concurrent jurisdiction in all cases arising under the constitution, laws, and treaties of the United States; and if a case of this description brought in a state court cannot be removed before judgment, nor revised after judgment, then the construction of the constitution, laws, and treaties of the United States is not confided particularly to their judicial department, but is confided equally to that department and to the state courts, however they may be constituted. "Thirteen independent courts," says a very celebrated statesman, (and we have now more than twenty such courts,) "of final jurisdiction over the same causes, arising upon the same laws, is a hydra in government, from which nothing but contradiction and confusion can proceed." . . .

We are not restrained, then, by the political relations between the general and state governments, from construing the words of the constitution, defining the judicial power, in their true sense. We are not bound to construe them more restrictively than they naturally import.

NATIONAL SUPREMACY AND FEDERALISM

McCulloch v. Maryland [3]

> *Probably the most celebrated and most cited of his opinions,* McCulloch v. Maryland *illustrates Marshall at the height of his powers. The case involved Congress's right to charter a national bank and whether the states might tax an agency of the national government. Marshall's use of the implied powers doctrine to sustain the bank charter is the classic expression of broad constitutional construction. Equally enduring, Marshall's rejection of the state bank tax has provided national agencies and institutions with protection from state interference.*

The first question made in the cause is—has congress power to incorporate a bank? It has been truly said, that this can scarcely be considered as an open question, entirely unprejudiced by the former proceedings of the nation respecting it. The principle now contested was introduced at a very early period of our history, has been recognised by many successive legislatures, and has been acted upon by the judicial department, in cases of peculiar delicacy, as a law of undoubted obligation. . . .

This government is acknowledged by all, to be one of enumerated powers. The principle, that it can exercise only the powers granted

[3] 4 Wheaton 316 (1819).

to it, would seem too apparent, to have required to be enforced by all those arguments, which its enlightened friends, while it was depending before the people, found it necessary to urge; that principle is now universally admitted. But the question respecting the extent of the powers actually granted, is perpetually arising, and will probably continue to arise, so long as our system shall exist. . . .

If any one proposition could command the universal assent of mankind, we might expect it would be this—that the government of the Union, though limited in its powers, is supreme within its sphere of action. This would seem to result, necessarily, from its nature. It is the government of all; its powers are delegated by all; it represents all, and acts for all. Though any one state may be willing to control its operations, no state is willing to allow others to control them. The nation, on those subjects on which it can act, must necessarily bind its component parts. . . . The government of the United States, then, though limited in its powers, is supreme; and its laws, when made in pursuance of the constitution, form the supreme law of the land, "anything in the constitution or laws of any state to the contrary notwithstanding."

Among the enumerated powers, we do not find that of establishing a bank or creating a corporation. But there is no phrase in the instrument which, like the articles of confederation, excludes incidental or implied powers; and which requires that everything granted shall be expressly and minutely described. Even the 10th amendment, which was framed for the purpose of quieting the excessive jealousies which had been excited, omits the word "expressly," and declares only, that the powers "not delegated to the United States, nor prohibited to the states, are reserved to the states or to the people;" thus leaving the question, whether the particular power which may become the subject of contest, has been delegated to the one government, or prohibited to the other, to depend on a fair construction of the whole instrument. The men who drew and adopted this amendment had experienced the embarrassments resulting from the insertion of this word in the articles of confederation, and probably omitted it, to avoid those embarrassments. A constitution, to contain an accurate detail of all the subdivisions of which its great powers will admit, and of all the means by which they may be carried into execution, would partake of the prolixity of a legal code, and could scarcely be embraced by the human mind. It would, probably, never be understood by the public. Its nature, therefore, requires, that only its great outlines should be marked, its important objects designated, and the minor ingredients which compose those objects, be deduced from the nature of the objects themselves. That this idea was entertained by the framers of the American constitution, is not only to be inferred from the nature of the instrument, but from the language. Why else were some of the limitations, found in the 9th section of the 1st article, introduced? It is also, in some degree, warranted, by their having omitted to use any restrictive term which might prevent its receiving a fair and just interpretation. In considering this question, then, we must never forget that it is a *constitution* we are expounding.

Although, among the enumerated powers of government, we do not find the word "bank" or "incorporation," we find the great powers, to lay and collect taxes; to borrow money; to regulate commerce; to declare and conduct a war; and to raise and support armies and navies. . . . Throughout this vast republic, from the St. Croix to the Gulf of Mexico, from the Atlantic to the Pacific, revenue is to be collected and expended, armies are to be marched and supported. The exigencies of the nation may require, that the treasure raised in the north should be transported to the south, that raised in the east, conveyed to the west, or that this order should be reversed. Is that construction of the constitution to be preferred, which would render these operations difficult, hazardous and expensive? Can we adopt that construction (unless the words imperiously require it), which would impute to the framers of that instrument, when granting these powers for the public good, the intention of impeding their exercise, by withholding a choice of means? If, indeed, such be the mandate of the constitution, we have only to obey; but that instrument does not profess to enumerate the means by which the powers it confers may be executed; nor does it prohibit the creation of a corporation, if the existence of such a being be essential, to the beneficial exercise of those powers. It is, then, the subject of fair inquiry, how far such means may be employed.

It is not denied, that the powers given to the government imply the ordinary means of execution. That, for example, of raising revenue, and applying it to national purposes, is admitted to imply the power of conveying money from place to place, as the exigencies of the nation may require, and of employing the usual means of conveyance. But it is denied, that the government has its choice of means; or, that it may employ the most convenient means, if, to employ them, it be necessary to erect a corporation. . . .

The power of creating a corporation, though appertaining to sovereignty, is not, like the power of making war, or levying taxes, or of regulating commerce, a great substantive and independent power, which cannot be implied as incidental to other powers, or used as a means of executing them. It is never the end for which other powers are exercised, but a means by which other objects are accomplished. No contributions are made to charity, for the sake of an incorporation, but a corporation is created to administer the charity; no seminary of learning is instituted, in order to be incorporated, but the corporate character is conferred to subserve the purposes of education. No city was ever built, with the sole object of being incorporated, but is incorporated as affording the best means of being well governed. The power of creating a corporation is never used for its own sake, but for the purpose of effecting something else. No sufficient reason is, therefore, perceived, why it may not pass as incidental to those powers which are expressly given, if it be a direct mode of executing them.

But the constitution of the United States has not left the right of congress to employ the necessary means, for the execution of the powers conferred on the government, to general reasoning. To its enumeration of powers is added, that of making "all laws which shall be necessary and proper, for carrying into execution the foregoing powers, and all other powers vested by this constitution, in the government of the United States, or in any department thereof." . . .

Congress is not empowered by it to make all laws, which may have relation to the powers conferred on the government, but such only as may be *"necessary and proper"* for carrying them into execution. The word *"necessary"* is considered as controlling the whole sentence, and as limiting the right to pass laws for the execution of the granted powers, to such as are indispensable, and without which the power would be nugatory. That it excludes the choice of means, and leaves to congress, in each case, that only which is most direct and simple. . . .

The result of the most careful and attentive consideration bestowed upon this clause is, that if it does not enlarge, it cannot be construed to restrain the powers of congress, or to impair the right of the legislature to exercise its best judgment in the selection of measures to carry into execution the constitutional powers of the government. If no other motive for its insertion can be suggested, a sufficient one is found in the desire to remove all doubts respecting the right to legislate on that vast mass of incidental powers which must be involved in the constitution, if that instrument be not a splendid bauble.

We admit, as all must admit, that the powers of the government are limited, and that its limits are not to be transcended. But we think the sound construction of the constitution must allow to the national legislature that discretion, with respect to the means by which the powers it confers are to be carried into execution, which will enable that body to perform the high duties assigned to it, in the manner most beneficial to the people. Let the end be legitimate, let it be within the scope of the constitution, and all means which are appropriate, which are plainly adapted to that end, which are not prohibited, but consist with the letter and spirit of the constitution, are constitutional. . . .

This clause, as construed by the state of Maryland, would abridge, and almost annihilate, this useful and necessary right of the legislature to select its means. That this could not be intended, is, we should think, had it not been already controverted, too apparent for controversy. . . .

Should congress, in the execution of its powers, adopt measures which are prohibited by the constitution; or should congress, under the pretext of executing its powers, pass laws for the accomplishment of objects not intrusted to the government; it would become the painful duty of this tribunal, should a case requiring such a decision come before it, to say that such an act was not the law of the land. But where the law is not prohibited, and is really calculated to effect any of the objects intrusted to the government, to undertake here to inquire into the decree of its necessity, would be to pass the line which circumscribes the judicial department, and to tread on legislative ground. This court disclaims all pretensions to such a power. . . .

It being the opinion of the court, that the act incorporating the bank is constitutional; and that the power of establishing a branch in the state of Maryland might be properly exercised by the bank itself, we proceed to inquire—

Whether the state of Maryland may, without violating the constitution, tax that branch? That the power of taxation is one of vital importance; that it is retained by the states; that it is not abridged by the grant of a similar power to the government of the Union; that it is to be concurrently exercised by the two governments—are truths which have never been denied. But such is the paramount character of the constitution, that its capacity to withdraw any subject from the action of even this power, is admitted. The states are expressly forbidden to lay any duties on imports or exports, except what may be absolutely necessary for executing their inspection laws. If the obligation of this prohibition must be conceded—if it may restrain a state from the exercise of its taxing power on imports and exports—the same paramount character would seem to restrain, as it certainly may restrain, a state from such other exercise of this power, as is in its nature incompatible with, and repugnant to, the constitutional laws of the Union. A law, absolutely repugnant to another, as entirely repeals that other as if express terms of repeal were used.

On this ground, the counsel for the bank place its claim to be exempted from the power of a state to tax its operations. There is no express provision for the case, but the claim has been sustained on a principle which so entirely pervades the constitution, is so intermixed with the materials which compose it, so interwoven with its web, so blended with its texture, as to be incapable of being separated from it, without rending it into shreds. This great principle is, that the constitution and the laws made in pursuance thereof are supreme; that they control the constitution and laws of the respective states, and cannot be controlled by them. From this, which may be almost termed an axiom, other propositions are deduced as corollaries, on the truth or error of which, and on their application to this case, the cause has been supposed to depend. These are, 1st. That a power to create implies a power to preserve: 2d. That a power to destroy, if wielded by a different hand, is hostile to, and incompatible with these powers to create and to preserve: 3d. That where this repugnancy exists, that authority which is supreme must control, not yield to that over which it is supreme. . . .

The power of congress to create, and of course, to continue, the bank, was the subject of the preceding part of this opinion; and is no longer to be considered as questionable. That the power of taxing it by the states may be exercised so as to destroy it, is too obvious to be denied. But taxation is said to be an absolute power, which acknowledges no other limits than those expressly prescribed in the constitution, and like sovereign power of every other description, is intrusted to the discretion of those who use it. . . .

That the power to tax involves the power to destroy; that the power to destroy may defeat and render useless the power to create; that there is a plain repugnance in conferring on one government a power to control the constitutional measures of another, which other, with respect to those very measures, is declared to be supreme over that which exerts the control, are propositions not to be denied. But all inconsistencies are to be reconciled by the magic of the word *confidence*. Taxation, it is said, does not necessarily and unavoidably destroy. To carry it to the excess of destruction, would be an abuse, to presume which, would banish that confidence which is essential to all government. But is this a case of confidence? Would the people of any one state trust those of another with a power to control the most insignificant operations of their state government? We know they would not. Why, then, should we suppose, that the people of any one state should be willing to trust those of another with a power to control the operations of a government to which they have confided their most important and most valuable interests? In the legislature of the Union alone, are all represented. The legislature of the Union alone, therefore, can be trusted by the people with the power of controlling measures which concern ,all, in the confidence that it will not be abused. This, then, is not a case of confidence, and we must consider it as it really is.

If we apply the principle for which the state of Maryland contends, to the constitution, generally, we shall find it capable of changing totally the character of that instrument. We shall find it capable of arresting all the measures of the government, and of prostrating it at the foot of the states. The American people have declared their constitution and the laws made in pursuance thereof, to be supreme; but this principle would transfer the supremacy, in fact, to the states. If the states may tax one instrument, employed by the government in the execution of its powers, they may tax any and every other instrument. . . . This was not intended by the American people. They did not design to make their government dependent on the states. . . .

The question is, in truth, a question of supremacy; and if the right of the states to tax the means employed by the general government be conceded, the declaration that the constitution, and the laws made in pursuance thereof, shall be the supreme law of the land, is empty and unmeaning declamation. . . .

The court has bestowed on this subject its most deliberate consideration. The result is a conviction that the states have no power, by taxation or otherwise, to retard, impede, burden, or in any manner control, the operations of the constitutional laws enacted by congress to carry into execution the powers vested in the general government. This is, we think, the unavoidable consequence of that supremacy which the constitution has declared. We are unanimously of opinion, that the law passed by the legislature of Maryland, imposing a tax on the Bank of the United States, is unconstitutional and void.

Weston v. Charleston[4]

Weston v. Charleston *extended further the* McCulloch *principle of intergovernmental immunities. The city of Charleston had levied a tax on federally issued bonds; Marshall found it obstructed the national power to borrow money. Maryland's bank tax had destructive purposes and tendencies; the Charleston tax on the other hand did not, but Marshall, nevertheless, held that it constituted an intolerable burden on the national government.*

The main question . . . is [whether] the stock issued for loans made to the government of the United States [is] liable to be taxed by states and corporations.

Congress has power "to borrow money on the credit of the United States." The stock it issues is the evidence of a debt created by the exercise of this power. The tax in question is a tax upon the contract subsisting between the government and the individual. It bears directly upon that contract, while subsisting and in full force. The power operates upon the contract the instant it is framed, and must imply a right to affect that contract. . . .

No one can be selected which is of more vital interest to the community than this of borrowing money on the credit of the United States. No power has been conferred by the American people on their government, the free and unburdened exercise of which more deeply affects every member of our republic. . . . Can anything be

---

[4] 2 Peters 449 (1829).

more dangerous, or more injurious, than the admission of a principle which authorizes every state and every corporation in the union, which possesses the right of taxation, to burden the exercise of this power at their discretion?

If the right to impose the tax exists, it is a right which in its nature acknowledges no limits. It may be carried to any extent, within the jurisdiction of the state or corporation which imposes it, which the will of each state and corporation may prescribe. A power which is given by the whole American people for their common good, which is to be exercised at the most critical periods for the most important purposes, on the free exercise of which the interest certainly, perhaps the liberty, of the whole may depend, may be burdened, impeded, if not arrested, by any of the organized parts of the confederacy.

In a society formed like ours with one supreme government for national purposes and numerous state governments for other purposes, in many respects independent and in the uncontrolled exercise of many important powers, occasional interferences ought not to surprise us. The power of taxation is one of the most essential to a state and one of the most extensive in its operation. The attempt to maintain a rule which shall limit its exercise is, undoubtedly, among the most delicate and difficult duties which can devolve on those whose province it is to expound the supreme law of the land in its application to the cases of individuals. This duty has more than once devolved on this Court. In the performance of it we have considered it as a necessary consequence from the supremacy of the government of the whole, that its action in the exercise of its legitimate powers should be free and unembarrassed by any conflicting powers in the possession of its parts; that the powers of a state cannot rightfully be so exercised as to impede and obstruct the free course of those measures which the government of the states united may rightfully adopt. . . .

A contract made by the government, in the exercise of its power, to borrow money on the credit of the United States, is, undoubtedly, independent of the will of any state in which the individual who lends may reside, and is, undoubtedly, an operation essential to the important objects for which the government was created. It ought, therefore, on the principles settled in the case of *M'Cullough* vs. *State of Maryland,* to be exempt from state taxation, and consequently from being taxed by corporations deriving their power from states. . . .

It is not the want of original power in an independent sovereign state, to prohibit loans to a foreign government, which restrains the legislature from direct opposition to those made by the United States. The restraint is imposed by our constitution. The American people have conferred the power of borrowing money on their government, and by making that government supreme, have shielded its action, in the exercise of this power, from the action of the local governments. The grant of the power is incompatible with a restraining or controlling power; and the declaration of supremacy is a declaration that no such restraining or controlling power shall be exercised. . . .

The tax on government stock is thought by this Court to be a tax on the contract, a tax on the power to borrow money on the credit of the United States, and, consequently, to be repugnant to the constitution.

We are, therefore, of opinion that the judgment of the constitutional court of the state of South Carolina, reversing the order made by the court of common pleas, awarding a prohibition to the city council of Charleston to restrain them from levying a tax imposed on six and seven per cent. stock of the United States, under an ordinance to raise supplies to the use of the city of Charleston for the year 1823, is erroneous in this; that the said constitutional court adjudged that the said ordinance was not repugnant to the constitution of the United States; whereas, this Court is of opinion that such repugnancy does exist. We are, therefore, of opinion that the said judgment ought to be reversed and annulled, and the cause remanded to the constitutional court for the state of South Carolina, that farther proceedings may be had therein according to law.

Barron v. Baltimore[5]

There were limits to Marshall's extension of nationalizing principles. In the case below, he refused to apply the guarantees of the first eight constitutional amendments against state action. The controversy involved a suit against the city to recover damages resulting from destruction of wharf property. Perhaps Marshall failed to extend the Bill of Rights amend-

[5] 7 Peters 243 (1833).

*ments because he was convinced of their original purpose as
limitations only upon the national government; perhaps, on
the other hand, he no longer could have carried the Court,
even if he had believed otherwise. Thirty-five years later, however, Marshall's opinion provided the impetus for passage of
the Fourteenth Amendment and the extension of the Bill of
Rights against state acts.*

The judgment brought up by this writ of error having been
rendered by the court of a State, this tribunal can exercise no jurisdiction over it, unless it be shown to come within the provisions of
the 25th section of the Judicial Act.

The plaintiff in error contends that it comes within that clause
in the 5th amendment to the constitution, which inhibits the taking
of private property for public use, without just compensation. He
insists that this amendment, being in favor of the liberty of the
citizen, ought to be so construed as to restrain the legislative power
of a State, as well as that of the United States. If this proposition be
untrue, the court can take no jurisdiction of the cause.

The question thus presented is, we think, of great importance, but
not of much difficulty.

The constitution was ordained and established by the people of
the United States for themselves, for their own government and not
for the government of the individual States. Each State established
a constitution for itself, and, in that constitution, provided such
limitations and restrictions on the powers of its particular government as its judgment dictated. The people of the United States
framed such a government for the United States as they supposed
best adapted to their situation, and best calculated to promote their
interests. The powers they conferred on this government were to be
exercised by itself; and the limitations on power, if expressed in
general terms, are naturally, and, we think, necessarily applicable
to the government created by the instrument. They are limitations
of power granted in the instrument itself; not of distinct governments, framed by different persons and for different purposes.

If these propositions be correct, the 5th amendment must be understood as restraining the power of the general government, not
as applicable to the States. In their several constitutions they have
imposed such restrictions on their respective governments as their

own wisdom suggested; such as they deemed most proper for themselves. It is a subject on which they judge exclusively, and with which others interfere no further than they are supposed to have a common interest. . . .

Had the people of the several States, or any of them, required changes in their constitutions; had they required additional safeguards to liberty from the apprehended encroachments of their particular governments; the remedy was in their own hands, and would have been applied by themselves. A convention would have been assembled by the discontented State, and the required improvements would have been made by itself. The unwieldy and cumbrous machinery of procuring a recommendation from two thirds of congress, and the assent of three fourths of their sister States, could never have occurred to any human being as a mode of doing that which might be effected by the State itself. Had the framers of these amendments intended them to be limitations on the powers of the state governments, they would have imitated the framers of the original constitution, and have expressed that intention. Had congress engaged in the extraordinary occupation of improving the constitutions of the several States by affording the people additional protection from the exercise of power by their own governments in matters which concerned themselves alone, they would have declared this purpose in plain and intelligible language.

But it is universally understood, it is a part of the history of the day, that the great revolution which established the constitution of the United States, was not effected without immense opposition. Serious fears were extensively entertained that those powers which the patriot statesmen, who then watched over the interests of our country, deemed essential to union, and to the attainment of those invaluable objects for which union was sought, might be exercised in a manner dangerous to liberty. In almost every convention by which the constitution was adopted, amendments to guard against the abuse of power were recommended. These amendments demanded security against the apprehended encroachments of the general government, not against those of the local governments.

In compliance with a sentiment thus generally expressed to quiet fears thus extensively entertained, amendments were proposed by the required majority in congress, and adopted by the States. These amendments contain no expression indicating an intention to apply them to the state governments. This court cannot so apply them.

We are of opinion that the provision in the 5th amendment to the constitution, declaring that private property shall not be taken for public use without just compensation, is intended solely as a limitation on the exercise of power by the government of the United States, and is not applicable to the legislation of the States. We are therefore of opinion, that there is no repugnancy between the several acts of the general assembly of Maryland, given in evidence by the defendants at the trial of this cause, in the court of that State, and the constitution of the United States. This court, therefore, has no jurisdiction of the cause; and it is dismissed.

ECONOMIC DEVELOPMENT: CONTRACTS AND COMMERCE

Fletcher v. Peck[6]

The contract clause of the Constitution (Article I, Section 10) basically reflected the belief during the 1780s that the national government must guarantee the sanctity of lawful debts and contracts against state interference. The notorious and complicated Yazoo land frauds first provided Marshall with an opportunity to implement the clause. In 1795, the Georgia legislature had granted the lands to several groups of speculators. But after disclosures that the legislators had been bribed, the land claims became an explosive political issue in the state and, eventually, throughout the nation. A newly elected legislature rescinded the grant in 1796. Meanwhile, the original grantees had sold their titles to speculators in other states. In the case below (a collusive one, incidentally), the claimants contended they were innocent investors and that the state had unconstitutionally impaired its contractual obligation.

That the legislature of Georgia, unless restrained by its own constitution, possesses the power of disposing of the unappropriated lands within its own limits, in such manner as its own judgment shall dictate, is a proposition not to be controverted. The only question, then, presented by this demurrer, for the consideration of the court, is this, did the then constitution of the State of Georgia prohibit the legislature to dispose of the lands, which were the subject of this contract, in the manner stipulated by the contract?

The question, whether a law be void for its repugnancy to the

6 Cranch 87 (1810).

constitution, is, at all times, a question of much delicacy, which ought seldom, if ever, to be decided in the affirmative, in a doubtful case. The court, when impelled by duty to render such a judgment, would be unworthy of its station, could it be unmindful of the solemn obligations which that station imposes. But it is not on slight implication and vague conjecture that the legislature is to be pronounced to have transcended its powers, and its acts to be considered as void. The opposition between the constitution and the law should be such that the judge feels a clear and strong conviction of their incompatibility with each other.

In this case the court can perceive no such opposition. In the constitution of Georgia, adopted in the year 1789, the court can perceive no restriction on the legislative power, which inhibits the passage of the act of 1795. They cannot say that, in passing that act, the legislature has transcended its powers, and violated the constitution. . . .

That corruption should find its way into the governments of our infant republics, and contaminate the very source of legislation, or that impure motives should contribute to the passage of a law, or the formation of a legislative contract, are circumstances most deeply to be deplored. How far a court of justice would, in any case, be competent, on proceedings instituted by the State itself, to vacate a contract thus formed, and to annul rights acquired, under that contract, by third persons having no notice of the improper means by which it was obtained, is a question which the court would approach with much circumspection. It may well be doubted how far the validity of a law depends upon the motives of its framers, and how far the particular inducements, operating on members of the supreme sovereign power of a State, to the formation of a contract by that power, are examinable in a court of justice. If the principle be conceded, that an act of the supreme sovereign power might be declared null by a court, in consequence of the means which procured it, still would there be much difficulty in saying to what extent those means must be applied to produce this effect. Must it be direct corruption, or would interest or undue influence of any kind be sufficient? Must the vitiating cause operate on a majority, or on what number of the members? Would the act be null, whatever might be the wish of the nation, or would its obligation or nullity depend upon the public sentiment?

If the majority of the legislature be corrupted, it may well be doubted, whether it be within the province of the judiciary to control their conduct, and, if less than a majority act from impure motives, the principle by which judicial interference would be regulated, is not clearly discerned.

Whatever difficulties this subject might present, when viewed under aspects of which it may be susceptible, this court can perceive none in the particular pleadings now under consideration.

This is not a bill brought by the State of Georgia, to annul the contract, nor does it appear to the court, by this count, that the State of Georgia is dissatisfied with the sale that has been made. The case, as made out in the pleadings, is simply this. One individual who holds lands in the State of Georgia, under a deed covenanting that the title of Georgia was in the grantor, brings an action of covenant upon this deed, and assigns, as a breach, that some of the members of the legislature were induced to vote in favor of the law, which constituted the contract, by being promised an interest in it, and that therefore the act is a mere nullity.

This solemn question cannot be brought thus collaterally and incidentally before the court. It would be indecent, in the extreme, upon a private contract, between two individuals, to enter into an inquiry respecting the corruption of the sovereign power of a State. If the title be plainly deduced from a legislative act, which the legislature might constitutionally pass, if the act be clothed with all the requisite forms of a law, a court, sitting as a court of law, cannot sustain a suit brought by one individual against another founded on the allegation that the act is a nullity, in consequence of the impure motives which influenced certain members of the legislature which passed the law. . . .

The lands in controversy vested absolutely in James Gunn and others, the original grantees, by the conveyance of the governor, made in pursuance of an act of assembly to which the legislature was fully competent. Being thus in full possession of the legal estate, they, for a valuable consideration, conveyed portions of the land to those who were willing to purchase. If the original transaction was infected with fraud, these purchasers did not participate in it, and had no notice of it. They were innocent. Yet the legislature of Georgia has involved them in the fate of the first parties to the transaction, and, if the act be valid, has annihilated their rights also.

The legislature of Georgia was a party to this transaction; and for a party to pronounce its own deed invalid, whatever cause may be assigned for its invalidity, must be considered as a mere act of power which must find its vindication in a train of reasoning not often heard in courts of justice.

But the real party, it is said, are the people, and when their agents are unfaithful, the acts of those agents cease to be obligatory. It is, however, to be recollected that the people can act only by these agents, and that, while within the powers conferred on them, their acts must be considered as the acts of the people. If the agents be corrupt, others may be chosen, and if their contracts be examinable, the common sentiment, as well as common usage of mankind, points out a mode by which this examination may be made, and their validity determined.

If the legislature of Georgia was not bound to submit its pretensions to those tribunals which are established for the security of property, and to decide on human rights, if it might claim to itself the power of judging in its own case, yet there are certain great principles of justice, whose authority is universally acknowledged, that ought not to be entirely disregarded.

If the legislature be its own judge in its own case, it would seem equitable that its decision should be regulated by those rules which would have regulated the decision of a judicial tribunal. The question was, in its nature, a question of title, and the tribunal which decided it was either acting in the character of a court of justice, and performing a duty usually assigned to a court, or it was exerting a mere act of power in which it was controlled only by its own will.

If a suit be brought to set aside a conveyance obtained by fraud, and the fraud be clearly proved, the conveyance will be set aside, as between the parties; but the rights of third persons, who are purchasers without notice, for a valuable consideration, cannot be disregarded. Titles, which, according to every legal test, are perfect, are acquired with that confidence which is inspired by the opinion that the purchaser is safe. If there be any concealed defect, arising from the conduct of those who had held the property long before he acquired it, of which he had no notice, that concealed defect cannot be set up against him. He has paid his money for a title good at law; he is innocent, whatever may be the guilt of others, and equity will not subject him to the penalties attached to that guilt. All titles would be insecure, and the intercourse between man and man would be very seriously obstructed, if this principle be over-turned.

A court of chancery, therefore, had a bill been brought to set aside the conveyance made to James Gunn and others, as being obtained by improper practices with the legislature, whatever might have been its decision as respected the original grantees, would have been bound, by its own rules, and by the clearest principles of equity, to leave unmolested those who were purchasers, without notice, for a valuable consideration.

If the legislature felt itself absolved from those rules of property which are common to all the citizens of the United States, and from those principles of equity which are acknowledged in all our courts, its act is to be supported by its power alone, and the same power may devest any other individual of his lands, if it shall be the will of the legislature so to exert it.

It is not intended to speak with disrespect of the legislature of Georgia, or of its acts. Far from it. The question is a general question, and is treated as one. For although such powerful objections to a legislative grant, as are alleged against this, may not again exist, yet the principle, on which alone this rescinding act is to be supported, may be applied to every case to which it shall be the will of any legislature to apply it. The principle is this: that a legislature may, by its own act, devest the vested estate of any man whatever, for reasons which shall, by itself, be deemed sufficient.

In this case the legislature may have had ample proof that the original grant was obtained by practices which can never be too much reprobated, and which would have justified its abrogation so far as respected those to whom crime was imputable. But the grant, when issued, conveyed an estate in fee-simple to the grantee, clothed with all the solemnities which law can bestow. This estate was transferable; and those who purchased parts of it were not stained by that guilt which infected the original transaction. Their case is not distinguishable from the ordinary case of purchasers of a legal estate without knowledge of any secret fraud which might have led to the emanation of the original grant. According to the well-known course of equity, their rights could not be affected by such fraud. Their situation was the same, their title was the same, with that of every other member of the community who holds land by regular conveyances from the original patentee.

Is the power of the legislature competent to the annihilation of such title, and to a resumption of the property thus held?

The principle asserted is, that one legislature is competent to repeal any act which a former legislature was competent to pass; and that one legislature cannot abridge the powers of a succeeding legislature.

The correctness of this principle, so far as respects general legislation, can never be controverted. But if an act be done under a law, a succeeding legislature cannot undo it. The past cannot be recalled by the most absolute power. Conveyances have been made, those conveyances have vested legal estates, and, if those estates may be seized by the sovereign authority, still, that they originally vested is a fact, and cannot cease to be a fact.

When, then, a law is in its nature a contract, when absolute rights have vested under that contract, a repeal of the law cannot devest those rights; and the act of annulling them, if legitimate, is rendered so by a power applicable to the case of every individual in the community.

It may well be doubted whether the nature of society and of government does not prescribe some limits to the legislative power; and if any be prescribed, where are they to be found, if the property of an individual, fairly and honestly acquired, may be seized without compensation.

The validity of this rescinding act, then, might well be doubted, were Georgia a single sovereign power. But Georgia cannot be viewed as a single, unconnected, sovereign power, on whose legislature no other restrictions are imposed than may be found in its own constitution. She is a part of a large empire; she is a member of the American Union; and that union has a constitution the supremacy of which all acknowledge, and which imposes limits to the legislatures of the several States, which none claim a right to pass. The constitution of the United States declares that no State shall pass any bill of attainder, *ex post facto* law, or law impairing the obligation of contracts.

Does the case now under consideration come within this prohibitory section of the constitution?

In considering this very interesting question, we immediately ask ourselves what is a contract? Is a grant a contract?

A contract is a compact between two or more parties, and is either executory or executed. An executory contract is one in which a party binds himself to do, or not to do, a particular thing; such was the law under which the conveyance was made by the governor. A contract executed is one in which the object of contract is performed; and this, says Blackstone, differs in nothing from a grant. The contract between Georgia and the purchasers was executed by the grant. A contract executed, as well as one which is executory, contains obligations binding on the parties. A grant, in its own nature, amounts to an extinguishment of the right of the grantor, and implies a contract not to reassert that right. A party is, therefore, always estopped by his own grant.

Since, then, in fact, a grant is a contract executed, the obligation of which still continues, and since the constitution uses the general term contract, without distinguishing between those which are executory and those which are executed, it must be construed to comprehend the latter as well as the former. A law annulling conveyances between individuals, and declaring that the grantors should stand seized of their former estates, notwithstanding those grants, would be as repugnant to the constitution as a law discharging the vendors of property from the obligation of executing their contracts by conveyances. It would be strange if a contract to convey was secured by the constitution, while an absolute conveyance remained unprotected.

If, under a fair construction of the constitution, grants are comprehended under the term contracts, is a grant from the State excluded from the operation of the provision? Is the clause to be considered as inhibiting the State from impairing the obligation of contracts between two individuals, but as excluding from that inhibition contracts made with itself?

The words themselves contain no such distinction. They are general, and are applicable to contracts of every description. If contracts made with the State are to be exempted from their operation, the exception must arise from the character of the contracting party, not from the words which are employed.

Whatever respect might have been felt for the state sovereignties, it is not to be disguised that the framers of the constitution viewed, with some apprehension, the violent acts which might grow out of the feelings of the moment; and that the people of the United States, in adopting that instrument, have manifested a determination to shield themselves and their property from the effects of those sudden and strong passions to which men are exposed. The restrictions on the legislative power of the States are obviously founded in this sentiment; and the Constitution of the United States contains what may be deemed a bill of rights for the people of each State.

No State shall pass any bill of attainder, *ex post facto* law, or law impairing the obligation of contracts.

A bill of attainder may affect the life of an individual, or may confiscate his property, or may do both.

In this form the power of the legislature over the lives and fortunes of individuals is expressly restrained. . . .

It is, then, the unanimous opinion of the court, that, in this case, the estate having passed into the hands of a purchaser for a valuable consideration, without notice, the State of Georgia was restrained, either by general principles which are common to our free institutions, or by the particular provisions of the Constitution of the United States, from passing a law whereby the estate of the plaintiff in the premises so purchased could be constitutionally and legally impaired and rendered null and void. . . .

Dartmouth College v. Woodward [7]

The Dartmouth College *case was Marshall's most influential contract clause case. Here, the chief justice equated corporate charters with contracts protected against state impairment by the Constitution. The decision served to assure private investors of the security of their holdings against arbitrary state action. But the decision had its pernicious effects, for it encouraged charter-seekers to pressure and bribe legislators for most favorable terms. Eventually, the states provided for "reserved power" clauses in their constitutions, general incorporation laws, or the specific charter; thus, they could alter, amend, or repeal charters as necessity dictated.*

The title of the plaintiffs originates in a charter, dated the 13th day of December, in the year 1769, incorporating twelve persons therein mentioned, by the name of "The Trustees of Dartmouth College," granting to them and their successors the usual corporate privileges and powers, and authorizing the trustees, who are to govern the college, to fill up all vacancies which may be created in their own body.

[7] 4 Wheaton 517 (1819).

The defendant claims under three acts of the legislature of New Hampshire, the most material of which was passed on the 27th of June, 1816, and is entitled, "An act to amend the charter, and enlarge and improve the corporation of Dartmouth College. . . ."

It can require no argument to prove, that the circumstances of this case constitute a contract. An application is made to the crown for a charter to incorporate a religious and literary institution. In the application it is stated, that large contributions have been made for the object, which will be conferred on the corporation, as soon as it shall be created. The charter is granted, and on its faith the property is conveyed. Surely, in this transaction, every ingredient of a complete and legitimate contract is to be found.

The points for consideration are,

1. Is this contract protected by the constitution of the United States?

2. Is it impaired by the acts under which the defendant holds? . . .

That the framers of the constitution did not intend to restrain the States in the regulation of their civil institutions, adopted for internal government, and that the instrument they have given us is not to be so construed, may be admitted. The provision of the constitution never has been understood to embrace other contracts than those which respect property, or some object of value, and confer rights which may be asserted in a court of justice. It never has been understood to restrict the general right of the legislature to legislate on the subject of divorces. Those acts enable some tribunal, not to impair a marriage contract, but to liberate one of the parties because it has been broken by the other. When any State legislature shall pass an act annulling all marriage contracts, or allowing either party to annul it without the consent of the other, it will be time enough to inquire whether such an act be constitutional. . . .

That education is an object of national concern, and a proper subject of legislation, all admit. That there may be an institution founded by government, and placed entirely under its immediate control, the officers of which would be public officers, amenable exclusively to government, none will deny. But is Dartmouth College such an institution? Is education altogether in the hands of government? Does every teacher of youth become a public officer, and do donations for the purpose of education necessarily become public property, so far that the will of the legislature, not the will of the donor, becomes the law of the donation? These questions are of serious moment to society, and deserve to be well considered.

Doctor Wheelock, as the keeper of his charity school, instructing the Indians in the art of reading, and in our holy religion; sustaining them at his own expense, and on the voluntary contributions of the charitable, could scarcely be considered as a public officer, exercising any portion of those duties which belong to government; nor could the legislature have supposed, that his private funds, or those given by others, were subject to legislative management, because they were applied to the purposes of education. When afterwards, his school was enlarged, and the liberal contributions made in England and in America, enabled him to extend his cares to the education of the youth of his own country, no change was wrought in his own character, or in the nature of his duties. Had he employed assistant tutors with the funds contributed by others, or had the trustees in England established a school, with Dr. Wheelock at its head, and paid salaries to him and his assistants, they would still have been private tutors; and the fact that they were employed in the education of youth, could not have converted them into public officers, concerned in the administration of public duties, or have given the legislature a right to interfere in the management of the fund. The trustees, in whose care that fund was placed by the contributors, would have been permitted to execute their trust, uncontrolled by legislative authority.

Whence, then, can be derived the idea, that Dartmouth College has become a public institution, and its trustees public officers, exercising powers conferred by the public, for public objects? Not from the source whence its funds were drawn; for its foundation is purely private and eleemosynary. Not from the application of those funds; for money may be given for education, and the persons receiving it do not, by being employed in the education of youth, become members of the civil government. Is it from the act of incorporation? Let this subject be considered.

A corporation is an artificial being, invisible, intangible, and existing only in contemplation of law. Being the mere creature of law, it possesses only those properties which the charter of its creation confers upon it, either expressly, or as incidental to its very existence. These are such as are supposed best calculated to effect the object for which it was created. Among the most important are immortality, and, if the expression may be allowed, individuality; properties by which a perpetual succession of many persons are considered as the same, and may act as a single individual. They enable a corporation to manage its own affairs, and to hold property without the perplexing intricacies, the hazardous and endless necessity of perpetual conveyances, for the purpose of transmitting it from hand to hand. It is chiefly for the purpose of clothing bodies of men, in succession, with these qualities and capacities, that corporations were invented, and are in use. By these means a perpetual succession of individuals are capable of acting for the promotion of the particular object, like one immortal being. But this being does not share in the civil government of the country, unless that be the purpose for which it was created. Its immortality no more confers on it political power, or a political character, than immortality would confer such power or character on a natural person. It is no more a State instrument, than a natural person exercising the same powers would be. If, then, a natural person, employed by individuals in the education of youth, or for the government of a seminary in which youth is educated, would not become a public officer, or be considered as a member of the civil government, how is it that this artificial being, created by law, for the purpose of being employed by the same individuals for the same purposes, should become a part of the civil government of the country? Is it because its existence, its capacities, its powers, are given by law? Because the government has given it the power to take and to hold property in a particular form, and for particular purposes, has the government a consequent right substantially to change that form, or to vary the purposes to which the property is to be applied? This principle has never been asserted or recognized, and is supported by no authority. Can it derive aid from reason?

The objects for which a corporation is created are universally such as the government wishes to promote. They are deemed beneficial to the country; and this benefit constitutes the consideration, and, in most cases, the sole consideration, of the grant. In most eleemosynary institutions, the object would be difficult, perhaps unattainable, without the aid of a charter of incorporation. Charitable, or public spirited individuals, desirous of making permanent appropriations for charitable or other useful purposes, find it impossible to effect their design, securely and certainly, without an incorporating act. They apply to the government, state their beneficent object, and offer to advance the money necessary for its accomplishment, provided the government will confer on the instrument, which is to execute their designs, the capacity to execute them. The proposition is considered and approved. The benefit to the public is considered as an ample compensation for the faculty it confers, and the corporation is created. If the advantages to the public constitute a full compensation for the faculty it gives, there can be no reason for exacting a further compensation, by claiming a right to exercise over this artificial being a power which changes its nature, and touches the fund, for the security and application of which it was created. There can be no reason for implying in a charter, given for a valuable consideration, a power which is not only not expressed, but is in direct contradiction to its express stipulations.

From the fact, then, that a charter of incorporation has been granted, nothing can be inferred which changes the character of the institution, or transfers to the government any new power over it. . . .

This is plainly a contract to which the donors, the trustees, and the crown (to whose rights and obligations New Hampshire succeeds) were the original parties. It is a contract made on a valuable consideration. It is a contract for the security and disposition of property. It is a contract, on the faith of which, real and personal estate has been conveyed to the corporation. It is then a contract within the letter of the constitution, and within its spirit also, unless the fact that the property is invested by the donors in trustees, for the promotion of religion and education, for the benefit of persons who are perpetually changing, though the objects remain the same, shall create a particular exception, taking this case out of the prohibition contained in the constitution.

It is more than possible that the preservation of rights of this description was not particularly in the view of the framers of the constitution, when the clause under consideration was introduced into that instrument. It is probable that interferences of more frequent recurrence, to which the temptation was stronger, and of which the mischief was more extensive, constituted the great motive for imposing this restriction on the State legislatures. But although a particular and a rare case may not, in itself, be of sufficient magnitude to induce a rule, yet it must be governed by the rule, when established, unless some plain and strong reason for excluding it can be given. It is not enough to say, that this particular case was not in the mind of the convention, when the article was framed, nor of the American people, when it was adopted. It is necessary to go further, and to say that, had this particular case been suggested, the language would have been so varied as to exclude it, or it would have been made a special exception. The case being within the words of the rule, must be within its operation likewise, unless there be something in the literal construction so obviously absurd or mischievous, or repugnant to the general spirit of the instrument, as to justify those who expound the constitution in making it an exception. . . .

The opinion of the court, after mature deliberation, is, that this is a contract, the obligation of which cannot be impaired, without violating the constitution of the United States. . . .

Ogden v. Saunders[8]

"The Supreme Conservative"—so Marshall's major biographer, Albert Beveridge, labeled him for his dissenting opinion in this case, in which a narrow majority of the Court barely sustained a state bankruptcy law applicable only to prospective contracts. Eight years earlier, in Sturges v. Crowinshield, *Marshall had carried a divided bench in rejecting a bankruptcy law that covered preexisting debts. The* Saunders *case provided the only occasion in which the chief justice publicly dissented in a constitutional law decision.*

It is well known that the court has been divided in opinion on this case. Three judges, Mr. Justice Duvall, Mr. Justice Story, and myself, do not concur in the judgment which has been pronounced. . . .

That there is an essential difference in principle between laws which act on past and those which act on future contracts; that those of the first description can seldom be justified, while those of the last are proper subjects of ordinary legislative discretion, must be admitted. A constitutional restriction, therefore, on the power to pass laws of the one class, may very well consist with entire legislative freedom respecting those of the other. Yet, when we consider the nature of our Union, that it is intended to make us, in a great measure, one people, as to commercial objects; that, so far as re-

[8] 12 Wheaton 213 (1827).

spects the intercommunication of individuals, the lines of separation between States are, in many respects, obliterated; it would not be matter of surprise if, on the delicate subject of contracts once formed, the interference of state legislation should be greatly abridged or entirely forbidden. . . .

The first paragraph of the tenth section of the first article, which comprehends the provision under consideration, contains an enumeration of those cases in which the action of the state legislature is entirely prohibited. . . .

In all . . . cases, whether the thing prohibited be the exercise of mere political power, or legislative action on individuals, the prohibition is complete and total. There is no exception from it. Legislation of every description is comprehended within it. A State is as entirely forbidden to pass laws impairing the obligation of contracts, as to make treaties, or coin money. The question recurs, what is a law impairing the obligation of contracts? . . .

No State shall "pass any law impairing the obligation of contracts." These words seem to us to import that the obligation is intrinsic, that it is created by the contract itself, not that it is dependent on the laws made to enforce it. When we advert to the course of reading generally pursued by American statesmen in early life, we must suppose that the framers of our constitution were intimately acquainted with the writings of those wise and learned men, whose treatises on the laws of nature and nations have guided public opinion on the subjects of obligation and contract. If we turn to those treatises, we find them to concur in the declaration that contracts possess an original intrinsic obligation, derived from the acts of free agents, and not given by government. We must suppose that the framers of our constitution took the same view of the subject, and the language they have used confirms this opinion. . . .

We cannot look back to the history of the times when the august spectacle was exhibited of the assemblage of a whole people by their representatives in convention, in order to unite thirteen independent sovereignties under one government, so far as might be necessary for the purposes of union, without being sensible of the great importance which was at that time attached to the 10th section of the 1st article. The power of changing the relative situation of debtor and creditor, of interfering with contracts, a power which comes home to every man, touches the interest of all, and controls the conduct of every individual in those things which he supposes to be proper for his own exclusive management, had been used to such an excess by the state legislatures as to break in upon the ordinary intercourse of society, and destroy all confidence between man and man. The mischief had become so great, so alarming, as not only to impair commercial intercourse, and threaten the existence of credit, but to sap the morals of the people and destroy the sanctity of private faith. To guard against the continuance of the evil was an object of deep interest with all the truly wise as well as the virtuous of this great community, and was one of the important benefits expected from a reform of the government.

To impose restraints on state legislation, as respected this delicate and interesting subject, was thought necessary by all those patriots who could take an enlightened and comprehensive view of our situation; and the principle obtained an early admission into the various schemes of government which were submitted to the convention. In framing an instrument, which was intended to be perpetual, the presumption is strong that every important principle introduced into it is intended to be perpetual also; that a principle expressed in terms to operate in all future time, is intended so to operate. But if the construction, for which the plaintiff's counsel contend, be the true one, the constitution will have imposed a restriction in language, indicating perpetuity, which every State in the Union may elude at pleasure. The obligation of contracts in force, at any given time, is but of short duration; and, if the inhibition be of retrospective laws only, a very short lapse of time will remove every subject on which the act is forbidden to operate, and make this provision of the constitution so far useless. Instead of introducing a great principle, prohibiting all laws of this obnoxious character, the constitution will only suspend their operation for a moment, or except from it preëxisting cases. The object would scarcely seem to be of sufficient importance to have found a place in that instrument. . . .

It is also worthy of consideration, that those laws which had effected all that mischief the constitution intended to prevent, were prospective as well as retrospective, in their operation. They embraced future contracts, as well as those previously formed. There is the less reason for imputing to the convention an intention, not manifested by their language, to confine a restriction intended to guard against the recurrence of those mischiefs, to retrospective legislation. . . .

Providence Bank v. Billings[9]

The Dartmouth College *doctrine unleashed extravagant claims for charter rights. Established interests demanded broad construction of charters, thus maximizing their assertions of privilege. In response to such pressure, states resorted to the reserved powers doctrine. In addition, strict judicial construction of charters helped to thwart such claims. In the* Providence Bank *case, the plaintiffs refused to pay a state bank tax enacted three decades after the charter had been granted. The bank contended that since its charter had no provision for taxation, the new levy impaired an implied contractual feature of immunity. Marshall dismissed the argument, and his narrow construction of the charter reflected his constant concern for sustaining governmental power and authority.*

It has been settled that a contract entered into between a State and an individual is as fully protected by the tenth section of the first article of the constitution as a contract between two individuals, and it is not denied that a charter incorporating a bank is a contract. Is this contract impaired by taxing the banks of the State?

This question is to be answered by the charter itself.

It contains no stipulation promising exemption from taxation. The State, then, has made no express contract which has been impaired by the act of which the plaintiffs complain. No words have been found in the charter, which, in themselves, would justify the opinion that the power of taxation was in the view of either of the parties, and that an exemption of it was intended, though not expressed. The plaintiffs find great difficulty in showing that the charter contains a promise, either express or implied, not to tax the bank. The elaborate and ingenious argument which has been urged amounts in substance to this. The charter authorizes the bank to employ its capital in banking transactions, for the benefit of the stockholders. It binds the State to permit these transactions for this object. Any law arresting directly the operations of the bank would violate this obligation, and would come within the prohibition of the constitution. But, as that cannot be done circuitously which may not be done directly, the charter restrains the State from passing any

9 4 Peters 514 (1830).

act which may indirectly destroy the profits of the bank. A power to tax the bank may unquestionably be carried to such an excess as to take all its profits, and still more than its profits, for the use of the State, and consequently destroy the institution. Now, whatever may be the rule of expediency, the constitutionality of a measure depends not on the degree of its exercise, but on its principle. A power, therefore, which may in effect destroy the charter, is inconsistent with it, and is impliedly renounced by granting it. Such a power cannot be exercised without impairing the obligation of the contract. When pushed to its extreme point, or exercised in moderation, it is the same power, and is hostile to the rights granted by the charter. This is substantially the argument for the bank. The plaintiffs cite and rely on several sentiments expressed on various occasions by this court, in support of these positions.

The claim of the Providence Bank is certainly of the first impression. The power of taxing moneyed corporations has been frequently exercised, and has never before, so far as is known, been resisted. Its novelty, however, furnishes no conclusive argument against it.

That the taxing power is of vital importance, that it is essential to the existence of government, are truths which it cannot be necessary to reaffirm. They are acknowledged and asserted by all. It would seem that the relinquishment of such a power is never to be assumed. We will not say that a State may not relinquish it, that a consideration sufficiently valuable to induce a partial release of it may not exist; but, as the whole community is interested in retaining it undiminished, that community has a right to insist that its abandonment ought not to be presumed in a case in which the deliberate purpose of the State to abandon it does not appear.

The plaintiffs would give to this charter the same construction as if it contained a clause exempting the bank from taxation on its stock in trade. But can it be supposed that such a clause would not enlarge its privileges? They contend that it must be implied, because the power to tax may be so wielded as to defeat the purpose for which the charter was granted. And may not this be said with equal truth of other legislative powers? Does it not also apply with equal force to every incorporated company? A company may be incorporated for the purpose of trading in goods as well as trading in money. If the policy of the State should lead to the imposition of a tax on unincorporated companies, could those which might be incorporated claim an exemption, in virtue of a charter which does not indicate such an intention? The time may come when a duty may be imposed on manufactures. Would an incorporated company be exempted from this duty, as the mere consequence of its charter?

The great object of an incorporation is to bestow the character and properties of individuality on a collective and changing body of men. This capacity is always given to such a body. Any privileges which may exempt it from the burdens common to individuals do not flow necessarily from the charter, but must be expressed in it, or they do not exist.

If the power of taxation is inconsistent with the charter, because it may be so exercised as to destroy the object for which the charter is given, it is equally inconsistent with every other charter, because it is equally capable of working the destruction of the objects for which every other charter is given. . . . Yet the power of taxation may be carried so far as to absorb these profits. Does this impair the obligation of the contract? The idea is rejected by all; and the proposition appears so extravagant, that it is difficult to admit any resemblance in the cases. And yet, if the proposition for which the plaintiffs contend be true, it carries us to this point. That proposition is, that a power which is in itself capable of being exerted to the total destruction of the grant, is inconsistent with the grant, and is therefore impliedly relinquished by the grantor, though the language of the instrument contains no allusion to the subject. If this be an abstract truth, it may be supposed universal. But it is not universal, and therefore its truth cannot be admitted, in these broad terms, in any case. We must look for the exemption in the language of the instrument; and if we do not find it there, it would be going very far to insert it by construction.

The power of legislation, and consequently of taxation, operates on all the persons and property belonging to the body politic. This is an original principle, which has its foundation in society itself. It is granted by all, for the benefit of all. It resides in government as part of itself, and need not be reserved when property of any description, or the right to use it in any manner, is granted to individuals or corporate bodies. However absolute the right of an individual may be, it is still in the nature of that right that it must bear a portion of the public burdens, and that portion must be determined by the legislature. This vital power may be abused; but the constitution of the United States was not intended to furnish the corrective for every abuse of power which may be committed by the state govern-ments. The interest, wisdom, and justice of the representative body, and its relations with its constituents, furnish the only security where there is no express contract, against unjust and excessive taxa-tion, as well as against unwise legislation generally. . . .

Gibbons v. Ogden[10]

The interstate trade wars and the consequent danger to de-velopment of a national market that marked the Confederation period provided the impetus for the commerce clause of the Constitution. This 1824 case first gave Marshall and his Su-preme Court colleagues an opportunity to interpret the mean-ing of the clause. (Marshall, however, had rendered an impor-tant commerce clause opinion in an 1820 circuit court de-cision.) Gibbons v. Ogden involved a confrontation between a New York state law providing steamboat monopoly privileges on its waters, including navigation between the state and New Jersey, and a steamboat license for the New York–New Jersey water route granted to Thomas Gibbons under authority of the Federal Coasting Act of 1793. Ogden, who held the mo-nopoly lease from Robert Fulton and Robert Livingston, ob-tained a state court injunction against Gibbons, and the latter subsequently appealed to the Supreme Court.

As preliminary to the very able discussions of the constitution which we have heard from the bar, and as having some influence on its construction, reference has been made to the political situation of these States, anterior to its formation. It has been said that they were sovereign, were completely independent, and were connected with each other only by a league. This is true. But, when these allied sovereigns converted their league into a government, when they converted their congress of ambassadors, deputed to deliberate on their common concerns, and to recommend measures of general utility, into a legislature, empowered to enact laws on the most in-teresting subjects, the whole character in which the States appear underwent a change, the extent of which must be determined by a fair consideration of the instrument by which that change was effected.

This instrument contains an enumeration of powers expressly

[10] 9 Wheaton 1 (1824).

granted by the people to their government. . . . We know of no rule for construing the extent of such powers, other than is given by the language of the instrument which confers them, taken in connection with the purposes for which they were conferred.

The words are: "Congress shall have power to regulate commerce with foreign nations, and among the several States, and with the Indian tribes."

The subject to be regulated is commerce; and our constitution being, as was aptly said at the bar, one of enumeration, and not of definition, to ascertain the extent of the power, it becomes necessary to settle the meaning of the word. The counsel for the appellee would limit it to traffic, to buying and selling, or the interchange of commodities, and do not admit that it comprehends navigation. This would restrict a general term, applicable to many objects, to one of its significations. Commerce, undoubtedly, is traffic, but it is something more: it is intercourse. It describes the commercial intercourse between nations, and parts of nations, in all its branches, and is regulated by prescribing rules for carrying on that intercourse. The mind can scarcely conceive a system for regulating commerce between nations, which shall exclude all laws concerning navigation, which shall be silent on the admission of the vessels of the one nation into the ports of the other, and be confined to prescribing rules for the conduct of individuals, in the actual employment of buying and selling, or of barter. . . .

The word used in the constitution, then, comprehends, and has been always understood to comprehend, navigation, within its meaning; and a power to regulate navigation is as expressly granted as if that term had been added to the word "commerce." . . .

We are now arrived at the inquiry—what is this power [to regulate commerce]?

It is the power to regulate; that is, to prescribe the rule by which commerce is to be governed. This power, like all others vested in congress, is complete in itself, may be exercised to its utmost extent, and acknowledges no limitations other than are prescribed in the constitution. These are expressed in plain terms, and do not affect the questions which arise in this case, or which have been discussed at the bar. If, as has always been understood, the sovereignty of congress, though limited to specified objects, is plenary as to those objects, the power over commerce with foreign nations, and among the several States, is vested in congress as absolutely as it would be in a single government, having in its constitution the same restrictions on the exercise of the power as are found in the constitution of the United States. . . .

But it has been urged with great earnestness that, although the power of congress to regulate commerce with foreign nations, and among the several States, be coextensive with the subject itself, and have no other limits than are prescribed in the constitution, yet the States may severally exercise the same power, within their respective jurisdictions. In support of this argument, it is said that they possessed it as an inseparable attribute of sovereignty, before the formation of the constitution, and still retain it, except so far as they have surrendered it by that instrument; that this principle results from the nature of the government, and is secured by the tenth amendment; that an affirmative grant of power is not exclusive, unless in its own nature it be such that the continued exercise of it by the former possessor is inconsistent with the grant, and that this is not of that description.

The appellant, conceding these postulates, except the last, contends that full power to regulate a particular subject, implies the whole power, and leaves no *residuum;* that a grant of the whole is incompatible with the existence of a right in another to any part of it. . . .

In our complex system, presenting the rare and difficult scheme of one general government, whose action extends over the whole, but which possesses only certain enumerated powers; and of numerous state governments, which retain and exercise all powers not delegated to the Union, contests respecting power must arise. Were it even otherwise, the measure taken by the respective governments to execute their acknowledged powers, would often be of the same description, and might, sometimes, interfere. This, however, does not prove that the one is exercising, or has a right to exercise, the powers of the other. . . .

Since, however, in exercising the power of regulating their own purely internal affairs, whether of trading or police, the States may sometimes enact laws, the validity of which depends on their interfering with, and being contrary to, an act of congress passed in pursuance of the constitution, the court will enter upon the inquiry, whether the laws of New York, as expounded by the highest tribunal of that State, have, in their application to this case, come into collision with an act of congress, and deprive a citizen of a right to which that act entitles him. Should this collision exist, it will be immaterial whether those laws were passed in virtue of a concurrent power "to regulate commerce with foreign nations and among the several States," or, in virtue of a power to regulate their domestic trade and police. In one case and the other, the acts of New York must yield to the law of congress; and the decision sustaining the privilege they confer, against a right given by a law of the Union, must be erroneous.

This opinion has been frequently expressed in this court, and is founded as well on the nature of the government as on the words of the constitution. In argument, however, it has been contended that, if a law passed by a State, in the exercise of its acknowledged sovereignty, comes into conflict with a law passed by congress in pursuance of the constitution, they affect the subject, and each other, like equal opposing powers.

But the framers of our constitution foresaw this state of things, and provided for it by declaring the supremacy not only of itself, but of the laws made in pursuance of it. The nullity of any act, inconsistent with the constitution, is produced by the declaration that the constitution is the supreme law. The appropriate application of that part of the clause which confers the same supremacy on laws and treaties, is to such acts of the state legislatures as do not transcend their powers, but, though enacted in the execution of acknowledged state powers, interfere with, or are contrary to the laws of congress, made in pursuance of the constitution, or some treaty made under the authority of the United States. In every such case, the act of congress, or the treaty, is supreme; and the law of the State, though enacted in the exercise of powers not controverted, must yield to it. . . .

But all inquiry into this subject seems to the court to be put completely at rest, by the act already mentioned, entitled, "An act for the enrolling and licensing of steam-boats."

This act authorizes a steam-boat employed, or intended to be employed, only in a river or bay of the United States, owned wholly or in part by an alien, resident within the United States, to be enrolled and licensed as if the same belonged to a citizen of the United States.

This act demonstrates the opinion of congress, that steam-boats may be enrolled and licensed, in common with vessels using sails.

They are, of course, entitled to the same privileges, and can no more be restrained from navigating waters, and entering ports which are free to such vessels, than if they were wafted on their voyage by the winds, instead of being propelled by the agency of fire. The one element may be as legitimately used as the other, for every commercial purpose authorized by the laws of the Union; and the act of a State inhibiting the use of either to any vessel having a license under the act of congress, comes, we think, in direct collision with that act. . . .

The conclusion to which we have come depends on a chain of principles which it was necessary to preserve unbroken; and, although some of them were thought nearly self-evident, the magnitude of the question, the weight of character belonging to those from whose judgment we dissent, and the argument at the bar, demanded that we should assume nothing.

Powerful and ingenious minds, taking as postulates that the powers expressly granted to the government of the Union, are to be contracted by construction into the narrowest possible compass, and that the original powers of the States are retained, if any possible construction will retain them, may, by a course of well-digested but refined and metaphysical reasoning founded on these premises, explain away the constitution of our country, and leave it a magnificent structure, indeed, to look at, but totally unfit for use. They may so entangle and perplex the understanding, as to obscure principles which were before thought quite plain, and induce doubts where, if the mind were to pursue its own course, none would be perceived. In such a case, it is peculiarly necessary to recur to safe and fundamental principles to sustain those principles, and, when sustained, to make them the tests of the arguments to be examined.

Willson v. Black Bird Creek Marsh Co.[11]

In Gibbons *v.* Ogden, *Marshall did not resolve the question of a concurrent role for state regulation of interstate commerce. The following case, like* Providence Bank, *illustrates Marshall's concern for a positive role by government, whether national or state. Delaware had authorized the defendant to build a dam across a navigable stream in order to improve marsh lands. Willson claimed that the dam obstructed a "common and public way" open to all citizens and thus conflicted with national authority to regulate commerce. Marshall's choices came down to favoring the latent, but unassumed,*

[11] 2 Peters 245 (1829).

*power of the national government, or to sanction the state's
action as a valid use of its police powers.*

The jurisdiction of the court being established, the more
doubtful question is to be considered, whether the act incorporating
the Black Bird Creek Marsh Company is repugnant to the constitution, so far as it authorizes a dam across the creek. The plea states
the creek to be navigable, in the nature of a highway, through which
the tide ebbs and flows.

The act of assembly by which the plaintiffs were authorized to
construct their dam, shows plainly that this is one of those many
creeks, passing through a deep level marsh adjoining the Delaware,
up which the tide flows for some distance. The value of the property
on its banks must be enhanced by excluding the water from the
marsh, and the health of the inhabitants probably improved. Measures calculated to produce these objects, provided they do not come
into collision with the powers of the general government, are undoubtedly within those which are reserved to the States. But the
measure authorized by this act stops a navigable creek, and must be
supposed to abridge the rights of those who have been accustomed
to use it. But this abridgment, unless it comes in conflict with the
constitution or a law of the United States, is an affair between the
government of Delaware and its citizens, of which this court can
take no cognizance.

The counsel for the plaintiffs in error insist that it comes in conflict with the power of the United States "to regulate commerce with
foreign nations and among the several States."

If congress had passed any act which bore upon the case; any act
in execution of the power to regulate commerce, the object of which
was to control state legislation over those small navigable creeks
into which the tide flows, and which abound throughout the lower
country of the middle and southern States; we should feel not much
difficulty in saying that a state law coming in conflict with such act
would be void. But congress has passed no such act. The repugnancy
of the law of Delaware to the constitution is placed entirely on its
repugnancy to the power to regulate commerce with foreign nations
and among the several States; a power which has not been so exercised as to affect the question.

We do not think that the act empowering the Blackbird Creek Marsh Company to place a dam across the creek, can, under all the circumstances of the case, be considered as repugnant to the power to regulate commerce in its dormant state, or as being in conflict with any law passed on the subject.

There is no error, and the judgment is affirmed.

PART TWO

JOHN MARSHALL VIEWED BY HIS CONTEMPORARIES

4

The Mind of the Chief Justice

WILLIAM WIRT [1]

William Wirt (1772–1834) generally is regarded as the out-standing constitutional lawyer of his day, Daniel Webster not-withstanding. Wirt argued his first case before the Supreme Court in 1816, and subsequently appeared in such cases as Dartmouth College, McCulloch v. Maryland, and Gibbons v. Ogden. Born in Maryland, Wirt later moved to Virginia, where he was admitted to the bar in 1790. He served Jefferson as prosecutor in the Burr trial in 1806. Monroe appointed him attorney general in 1817, and he remained in that post through the end of John Quincy Adams's presidential term in 1829. Wirt's comments on Chief Justice Marshall originally appeared in the Virginia Argus *in August and September, 1803.*

The [Chief Justice] . . . of the United States is, in his person, tall, meager, emaciated; his muscles relaxed, and his joints so loosely connected, as not only to disqualify him, apparently, for any vigorous exertion of body, but to destroy every thing like elegance and harmony in his air and movements. Indeed, in his whole appearance, and demeanour; dress, attitudes, gesture; sitting, standing or walking; he is as far removed from the idolized graces of lord Chesterfield, as any other gentleman on earth. To continue the portrait: his head and face are small in proportion to his height; his complexion swarthy; the muscles of his face, being relaxed, give him the ap-

---

[1] William Wirt, *Letters of the British Spy,* 10th ed. (New York, 1832), 178–84.

pearance of a man of fifty years of age, nor can he be much younger; his countenance has a faithful expression of great good humour and hilarity; while his black eyes—that unerring index—possess an irradiating spirit, which proclaims the imperial powers of the mind that sits enthroned within.

This extraordinary man, without the aid of fancy, without the advantages of person, voice, attitude, gesture, or any of the ornaments of an orator, deserves to be considered as one of the most eloquent men in the world; if eloquence may be said to consist in the power of seizing the attention with irresistible force, and never permitting it to elude the grasp, until the hearer has received the conviction which the speaker intends.

As to his person, it has already been described. His voice is dry, and hard; his attitude, in his most effective orations, was often extremely awkward; as it was not unusual for him to stand with his left food in advance, while all his gesture proceeded from his right arm, and consisted merely in a vehement, perpendicular swing of it, from about the elevation of his head, to the bar, behind which he was accustomed to stand.

As to fancy, if she hold a seat in his mind at all, which I very much doubt, his gigantic genius tramples with disdain, on all her flower-decked plats and blooming parterres. How then, you will ask, with a look of incredulous curiosity, how is it possible that such a man can hold the attention of an audience enchained, through a speech of even ordinary length? I will tell you.

He possesses one original, and, almost, supernatural faculty; the faculty of developing a subject by a single glance of his mind, and detecting at once, the very point on which every controversy depends. No matter what the question: though ten times more knotty than "the gnarled oak," the lightning of heaven is not more rapid nor more resistless, than his astonishing penetration. Nor does the exercise of it seem to cost him an effort. On the contrary, it is as easy as vision. I am persuaded that his eyes do not fly over a landscape and take in its various objects with more promptitude and facility, than his mind embraces and analyzes the most complex subject.

Possessing while at the bar this intellectual elevation, which enabled him to look down and comprehend the whole ground at once, he determined immediately and without difficulty, on which side the question might be most advantageously approached and assailed. In a bad cause his art consisted in laying his premises so remotely from the point directly in debate, or else in terms so general and so specious, that the hearer, seeing no consequence which could be drawn from them, was just as willing to admit them as not; but his premises once admitted, the demonstration, however distant, followed as certainly, as cogently, as inevitably, as any demonstration in Euclid.

All his eloquence consists in the apparently deep self-conviction, and emphatic earnestness of his manner; the correspondent simplicity and energy of his style; the close and logical connexion of his thoughts; and the easy gradations by which he opens his lights on the attentive minds of his hearers.

The audience are never permitted to pause for a moment. There is no stopping to weave garlands of flowers, to hang in festoons, around a favourite argument. On the contrary, every sentence is progressive; every idea sheds new light on the subject; the listener is kept perpetually in that sweetly pleasurable vibration, with which the mind of man always receives new truths; the dawn advances in easy but unremitting peace; the subject opens gradually on the view; until, rising in high relief, in all its native colours and proportions, the argument is consummated, by the conviction of the delighted hearer. . . .

His political adversaries allege that he is a mere lawyer; that his mind has been so long trammelled by judicial precedent, so long habituated to the quart and tierce of forensic digladiation, (as doctor Johnson would probably have called it,) as to be unequal to the discussion of a great question of state. . . .

Indeed, if the objection to [Marshall] . . . mean any thing more than that he has not had the same illumination and exercise in matters of state as if he had devoted his life to them, I am unwilling to admit it. The force of a cannon is the same, whether pointed at a rampart or a man of war, although practice may have made the engineer more expert in the one case than in the other. So it is clear, that practice may give a man a greater command over one class of subjects than another; but the inherent energy of his mind remains the same, whithersoever it may be directed. From this impression I have never seen any cause to wonder at what is called a universal genius: it proves only that the man has applied a powerful mind to the consideration of a great variety of subjects, and pays a compliment rather to his superior industry, than his superior intellect. I am very certain that the gentleman of whom we are speaking, possesses the *acumen* which might constitute him a universal genius, according to the usual acceptation of the phrase. But if he be the truant, which his warmest friends represent him to be, there is very little probability that he will ever reach this distinction.

CHARLES AUGUSTUS MURRAY [2]

The following selection is from a travel account of an Englishman who incidentally was the grandson of Lord Dunmore, the last royal governor of Virginia. Murray visited the chief justice a few months before Marshall's death in 1835.

Judge Marshall, who is Chief Justice of the Supreme Court, and, in fact, Lord Chancellor of the United States, is one of the most remarkable and distinguished men that has adorned the legislature of either shore of the Atlantic. He began life as a soldier; and, during the American war, served in the militia, where he rose to the rank of General: after which he came to the bar, and passed through all its gradations to his present high situation, which is, in my opinion, the proudest that an American can enjoy, not excepting that of President; inasmuch as it is less subject "arbitrio popularis auræ;" and as the court over which he presides can affirm and decide what is and what is not the constitution of the United States. The judge is a tall venerable man, about eighty years of age, his hair tied in a cue, according to olden custom, and with a countenance indicating that simplicity of mind and benignity which so eminently distinguish his character. As a judge he has no rival, his knowledge being profound, his judgment clear and just, and his quickness in apprehending either the fallacy or truth of an argument as surprising. I had the pleasure of several long conversations with him, and was struck with admiration at the extraordinary union of modesty and power, gentleness and force, which his mind displays. What he knows he communicates without reserve; he speaks with a clearness of expression, and in a tone of simple truth, which compel conviction; and on all subjects on which his knowledge is not *certain,* or which admit of doubt or argument, he delivers his opinion

[2] Charles Augustus Murray, *Travels in North America,* 2 vols. (London, 1841) 2: 158–60.

with a candid diffidence, and with a deference for that of others, amounting almost to timidity: still, it is a timidity which would disarm the most violent opponent, and win respect and credence from any auditor. I remember having often observed a similar characteristic attributed to the immortal Newton. The simplicity of his character is not more singular than that of his life; pride, ostentation, and hypocrisy are "Greek to him;" and he really lives up to the letter and spirit of republicanism, while he maintains all the dignity due to his age and office.

His house is small, and more humble in appearance than those of the average of successful lawyers or merchants. I called three times upon him; there is no bell to the door: once I turned the handle of it, and walked in unannounced; on the other two occasions he had seen me coming, and had lifted the latch and received me at the door, although he was at the time suffering from some very severe contusions received in the stage while travelling on that road from Fredericsburgh to Richmond, which I have before described. I verily believe there is not a particle of vanity in his composition, unless it be of that venial and hospitable nature which induces him to pride himself on giving to his friends the best glass of Madera in Virginia. In short, blending, as he does, the simplicity of a child and the plainness of a republican with the learning and ability of a lawyer, the venerable dignity of his appearance would not suffer in comparison with that of the most respected and distinguished-looking peer in the British House of Lords.

5

The Critics: Federalist Extremists

Marshall's relations with his fellow Federalists always were ambiguous. His relationship with Washington certainly enhanced his reputation within the party, but many of the more conservative New Englanders never really accepted him. As party differences hardened near the end of Adams's administration in the 1790s, the gap widened between Marshall and the extremists. They never forgave him for his opposition to the Sedition Act and his loyalty to the president. Indeed, his appointment as chief justice came as a blow to the extremists, who favored Associate Justice William Paterson. The following selections reflect the wariness and distrust of Marshall by his Federalist detractors. It is ironic how they so misjudged Marshall's view of constitutional interpretation.

OLIVER WOLCOTT [1]

A number of distinguished men appear from the southward, who are not pledged by any act to support the system of the last Congress; these men will pay great respect to the opinions of General Marshall; he is doubtless a man of virtue and distinguished talents, but he will think much of the State of Virginia, and is too much disposed to govern the world according to rules of logic; he will read and expound the constitution as if it were a penal statute, and will sometimes be embarassed with doubts of which his friends will not perceive the importance.

[1] Wolcott to Fisher Ames, December 29, 1799. George Gibbs, ed., *Memoirs of the Administrations of Washington and John Adams Edited from the Papers of Oliver Wolcott*, 2 vols. (New York, 1846), 2: 314.

THEODORE SEDGWICK [2]

We have, it is true, enacted a bankrupt law—a measure, in my belief, of considerable importance; but it is far from being such an one as I wished. The *acts* in curing bankruptcy are too restricted, and the trial of the question Bankrupt or not, by jury, will be found inconvenient, embarrassing, & dilatory. This mischief was occasioned by Virginia Theory. It was the whim of General Marshall; with him a *sine qua non* of assent to the measure, & without him the bill must have been lost, for it passed the House by my casting vote. Besides the bankrupt bill, we have passed one more of great importance. It makes it the *Duty* of the Secry. of the Treasury, at the commencement of a session, to report to the Legislature on all the subjects of revenue & finance. This will give splendor to the officer and respectability to the executive Department of Govt. Besides these two laws, all the rest we have made are, as to any permanently beneficial effects, hardly worth the parchment on which they are written. The reason of this feebleness is a real feebleness of character in the house. Marshall was looked up to as the man whose great and commanding genius was to enlighten & direct the national councils. This was the general sentiment, while some, and those of no inconsiderable importance, calculating on his foolish declaration, relative to the alien & sedition laws, thought him temporizing, while others deemed him feeble. None had in my opinion justly appreciated his character. As his character has stamped itself on the measures of the present session, I am desirous of letting you know how I view it. He is a man of a very affectionate disposition, of great simplicity of manners and honest & honorable in all his conduct. He is attached to pleasures, with convivial habits strongly fixed. He is indolent, therefore, and indisposed to take part in the common business of the house. He has a strong attachment to popularity but indisposed to sacrifice to it his integrity; hence it is that he is disposed on all popular subjects to feel the public pulse and hence results indecision and *an expression* of doubt. Doubts suggested by him create in more feeble minds those which are irremovable. He is disposed to the erotic refinement, and to express great respect for the sovereign people, and to quote their opinions as an evidence of truth. The latter is of all things the most destructive of personal independence & of

[2] Sedgwick to Rufus King, May 11, 1800. Charles R. King, ed., *The Life and Correspondence of Rufus King*, vol. 3 (New York, 1896), pp. 236–38.

that weight of character which a great man ought to possess. This gentleman, when aroused, has strong reasoning powers; they are indeed almost unequalled. But before they are excited, he has frequently, nearly, destroyed any impression from them. I will give you an instance which will render this observation perfectly intelligible.

Looking forward to the ensuing election, it was deemed indispensable to prescribe a mode for canvassing the votes, provided there should be a dispute. There being no law in the state, the governor had declined, and the jacobins propagated the report, that he would call on the people, by proclamation, to choose electors, & that he would return their votes. A bill was brought into the Senate & passed, wisely & effectually providing against the evil, by the constitution of a committee with ultimate powers of decision. Mr. Marshall in the first place called in question the constitutional powers of the legislature to delegate such authority to a Committee. On this question I had a long conversation with him, & he finally confessed himself (for there is not a more candid man on earth) to be convinced. He then resorted to another ground of opposition. He said the people having authorized the members to decide, personally, all disputes relative to those elections, altho' the power was not indelegable, yet he thought, in its nature, it was too delicate to be delegated, untill experience had demonstrated that great inconveniences would attend its exercise by the Legislature; altho' he had no doubt such would be the result of the attempt. This objection is so attenuated and unsubstantial as to be hardly perceivable by a mind so merely practical as mine. He finally was convinced that it was so and abandoned it. In the mean time, however, he had dwelt so much, in conversation, on these subjects that he had dissipated our majority, and it never could again be compacted. The consequence was that the bill was lost.

6

The Critics: Jeffersonians and Jacksonians

THOMAS JEFFERSON

The following selections from Thomas Jefferson's correspondence briefly trace the development of his opposition to Marshall. Beginning with the incipient partisan struggles of the 1790s, Jefferson's comments consistently reflected both his hostility and frustration toward Marshall. In these letters, Jefferson assaulted his fellow Virginian for his "English principles," his "hypocrisy" as a republican, his "crafty" domination of the Supreme Court, and the "impropriety" and "extrajudicial" character of his opinions.

Jefferson to James Madison, November 26, 1795 [1]

Though Marshall will be able to embarrass the republican party in the assembly a good deal, yet upon the whole, his having gone into it will be of service. He has been hitherto able to do more mischief acting under the mask of Republicanism than he will be able to do after throwing it plainly off. His lax lounging manners have made him popular with the bulk of the people of Richmond, & a profound hypocrisy with many thinking men of our country. But having come forth in the plenitude of his English principles the latter will see that it is high time to make him known.

Jefferson to Thomas Ritchie, December 25, 1820 [2]

The judiciary of the United States is the subtle corps of sappers and miners constantly working under ground to undermine

[1] Paul L. Ford, ed., *Writings of Thomas Jefferson* (New York: The Macmillan Company, 1905), 8: 197–98.
[2] Ford, ed., *Writings of Jefferson*, 12: 177–78.

the foundations of our confederated fabric. They are construing our constitution from a co-ordination of a general and special government to a general and supreme one alone. This will lay all things at their feet, and they are too well versed in English law to forget the maxim, *"boni judicis est ampliare jurisdictionem."* We shall see if they are bold enough to take the daring stride their five lawyers have lately taken. If they do, then, with the editor of our book, in his address to the public, I will say, that "against this every man should raise his voice," and more, should uplift his arm. Who wrote this admirable address? Sound, luminous, strong, not a word too much, nor one which can be changed but for the worse. That pen should go on, lay bare these wounds of our constitution, expose the decisions *seriatim,* and arouse, as it is able, the attention of the nation to these bold speculators on its patience. Having found, from experience, that impeachment is an impracticable thing, a mere scare-crow, they consider themselves secure for life; they sculk from responsibility to public opinion, the only remaining hold on them, under a practice first introduced into England by Lord Mansfield. An opinion is huddled up in conclave, perhaps by a majority of one, delivered as if unanimous, and with the silent acquiescence of lazy or timid associates, by a crafty chief judge, who sophisticates the law to his mind, by the turn of his own reasoning. A judiciary law was once reported by the Attorney General to Congress, requiring each judge to deliver his opinion *seriatim* and openly, and then to give it in writing to the clerk to be entered in the record. A judiciary independent of a king or executive alone, is a good thing; but independence of the will of the nation is a solecism, at least in a republican government.

Jefferson to William Johnson, June 12, 1823 [3]

You request me confidentially, to examine the question, whether the Supreme Court has advanced beyond its constitutional limits, and trespassed on those of the State authorities? . . . On the decision of the case of Cohens *vs.* The State of Virginia, in the Supreme Court of the United States, in March, 1821, Judge Roane, under the signature of Algernon Sidney, wrote for the *Enquirer* a series of papers on the law of that case. I considered these papers maturely as they came out, and confess that they appeared to me to

[3] Ford, ed., *Writings of Jefferson,* 12: 254–59.

pulverize every word which had been delivered by Judge Marshall, of the extra-judicial part of his opinion; and all was extra-judicial, except the decision that the act of Congress had not purported to give to the corporation of Washington the authority claimed by their lottery law, of controlling the laws of the States within the States themselves. But unable to claim that case, he could not let it go entirely, but went on gratuitously to prove, that notwithstanding the eleventh amendment of the constitution, a State *could* be brought as a defendant, to the bar of his court; and again, that Congress might authorize a corporation of its territory to exercise legislation within a State, and paramount to the laws of that State. I cite the sum and result only of his doctrines, according to the impression made on my mind at the time, and still remaining. If not strictly accurate in circumstance, it is so in substance. This doctrine was so completely refuted by Roane, that if he can be answered, I surrender human reason as a vain and useless faculty, given to bewilder, and not to guide us. . . .

This practice of Judge Marshall, of travelling out of his case to prescribe what the law would be in a moot case not before the court, is very irregular and very censurable. I recollect another instance, and the more particularly, perhaps, because it in some measure bore on myself. Among the midnight appointments of Mr. Adams, were commissions to some federal justices of the peace for Alexandria. These were signed and sealed by him, but not delivered. I found them on the table of the department of State, on my entrance into office, and I forbade their delivery. Marbury, named in one of them, applied to the Supreme Court for a mandamus to the Secretary of State, (Mr. Madison) to deliver the commission intended for him. The court determined at once, that being an original process, they had no cognizance of it; and therefore the question before them was ended. But the Chief Justice went on to lay down what the law would be, had they jurisdiction of the case, to wit: that they should command the delivery. The object was clearly to instruct any other court having the jurisdiction, what they should do if Marbury should apply to them. Besides the impropriety of this gratuitous interference, could anything exceed the perversion of law? For if there is any principle of law never yet contradicted, it is that delivery is one of the essentials to the validity of the deed. Although signed and sealed, yet as long as it remains in the hands of the party himself, it is in *fieri* only, it is not a deed, and can be made so only by its delivery. In the hands of a third person it may be made an escrow. But whatever is in the executive offices is certainly deemed to be in the hands of the President; and in this case, was actually in my hands, because, when I countermanded them, there was as yet no Secretary of State. Yet this case of Marbury and Madison is continually cited by bench and bar, as if it were settled law, without any animadversion on its being merely an *obiter* dissertation of the Chief Justice. . . .

I rejoice in the example you set of *seriatim* opinions. I have heard it often noticed, and always with high approbation. Some of your brethren will be encouraged to follow it occasionally, and in time, it may be felt by all as a duty, and the sound practice of the primitive court be again restored. Why should not every judge be asked his opinion, and give it from the bench, if only by yea or nay? Besides ascertaining the fact of his opinion, which the public have a right to know, in order to judge whether it is impeachable or not, it would show whether the opinions were unanimous or not, and thus settle more exactly the weight of their authority.

WILLIAM BRANCH GILES [4]

Jefferson's congressional lieutenants during his presidency regularly echoed their leader's sentiments toward Marshall. During the debates on the repeal of the Judiciary Act of 1801 and the impeachment trial of Samuel Chase, radical Republicans attacked Marshall and his Federalist colleagues, often hinting that the chief justice was a possible target for impeachment. Perhaps no action of Marshall's rankled these Republicans more at this time than his handling of Aaron Burr's treason trial. Jefferson's close ally, Virginia Senator William B. Giles charged that Marshall's behavior betrayed judicial independence and that it unmasked his partisan aims.

The retina of the human mind is not fit parchment for the transcription of laws. It is too much like changeable silk. It may vary its complexion, especially when held up to political sunshine. He begged the Senate to take a view of the judicial proceedings which

---

[4] *Annals of Congress*, 10th Cong., 1st sess., February 11, 1808, pp. 125–26.

had taken place in the United States in relation to this subject [i.e., Burr's treason trial]. . . .

These judicial results appeared strange to him, and he believed they did to every impartial man in the United States. He did not mean to infer from these circumstances anything more than that the highest judicial officers were not exempt from the frailties and feelings of human nature; nor did he mean to use them for the purpose of detracting one atom of independence from the judges; very far from it. He wished they were more independent than he feared they were. But he entertained a very different opinion of the honorable and dignified character of an independent judge; of a department in some respects dependent, and of a judge, who, forgetting the nature of his office, is perpetually aspiring not only to render his department absolutely independent, but to render it supreme over all the other departments of the Government; in the one case he is placed in the elevated and dignified attitude of distributing justice impartially among his fellow-citizens; in the other, he is reduced to the miserable political intriguer, scrambling for power; for when once this appetite for power is indulged, the sacred mantle of the judicial character will be found but a feeble barrier against its influence. There was nothing in names—it was not material whether they were called judges, or consuls, or censors—once place power before their eyes, and they would all, with an equal impulse, pursue the means best calculated to attain it. This is human nature; and, under such circumstances, raise this sacred mantle of the judge, and you will find concealed beneath it strong marks of the frailties common to human nature. Hence this argument, derived from the sacredness of the judicial character, had but little influence on his mind; and therefore could never be an inducement for him to yield to their claims to ultimate and unlimited powers; even the oaths taken by the judges have been suggested by them as arguments in favor of their claims to the ultimate power of the Government. Without seeming to recollect that their number is seven, and that the same oath is taken by above one hundred and seventy members of both Houses of Congress; and, as a further protection of the Constitution, Congress is composed of two branches, placed as mutual checks on each other.

NILES' WEEKLY REGISTER [5]

*Despite the animosity and influence of the Jeffersonians,
few of the Marshall Court's decisions before 1819 aroused
significant reactions. But, thereafter, attacks on the Court
sharply increased as the gap widened between sectional interests and Marshall's views of national power and public
policy. The chief justice's opinion sustaining the national bank
and his broad construction of national powers in McCulloch
v. Maryland (1819) provoked a renewed emphasis on state
sovereignty doctrines, particularly from Southern, or Southern-
oriented, spokesmen.*

An insidious dilapidation or violent dismemberment of the
American union, together with a consolidation of the reserved rights
and powers of the states, is the darling hope that the enemies of
liberty, at home and abroad, have hugged to their heart with
demoniac fervor and constancy. They have hated and still hate, the
freedom of the people of the United States, on the principles with
which Satan regarded the happy condition of our first parents in
the garden of Eden—their own perverse dispositions not being fitted
to participate in an equality of rights, or their inordinate pride
rejecting every measure calculated to do away distinctions among
men, save in virtue and usefulness. No part of our editorial duty has
been performed with more alacrity than to combat with such, and
to encourage a confidence in the perpetuity of the confederacy, in its
present super-excellent form—to descant upon the inestimable advantages that must flow from a well-balanced system, with an honest
administration of its principles for the common good; shewing how
every part transmitted intelligence and strength to a general point,
from whence the collected wisdom of the nation, with collected
force, was re-transmitted to benefit every part of the common family.
But, we always contended that the *living principle* was in the virtue
of the people, and the sovereignty of the states—and that these were
so closely united in giving order to the system, that neither could be
dispensed with. The *individuals* of this country having, by the favor
of Providence, and patience and perseverance, worked out their

[5] March 13, 1819, 16: 41, 43, 44.

emancipation from British despotism, gave up to their state governments certain of their rights for the better preservation of those that they thought proper to retain; and the states, in like manner and for like purposes, agreed to establish a national head, to direct the *general* affairs of the confederation, in peace and in war. Here was a system that we confidently trusted was to confer happiness on many millions of freemen, to the thousandth generation. We discovered nothing which had happened to jeopardize this most splendid inheritance—and never suffered the idea to prevail that the RESERVED rights of the people, or of the states, could be *seriously* compromitted by any act of the national administration, trusting in the virtue of the *ballot* to reform abuses and punish those guilty of them. It was that thus influenced, we have labored so faithfully to build up a NATIONAL CHARACTER, to inspire a *home feeling,* a proud and jealous regard of our rights as men—rights which the people, in obedience to the will of GOD who created them free, cannot legally transfer to the keeping of others. We were aware, nevertheless, of the intrigues of the ambitious and corrupt, and had partially estimated the growing power of the rich and avaricious. We knew that few men were able to restrain, as they ought, any degree of authority which they might acquire over their fellow beings, or apply the compass to prescribe a line beyond which their unruly passions should not pass; still, we thought such might be checked, confused, and dismissed, by a redeeming spirit in the people, to whom *all* were accountable for their conduct in the public affairs.

Having so long entertained such opinions as incontrovertible truths, and as a weak, but honest apostle in the cause of mankind, endeavored to impress them upon all within our reach, the horror of an apprehension that we have deceived ourselves and others, may be better felt than described: it is like to a man discovering the infidelity of his wife whilst she reposes on his bosom, and heart seems united to heart! A deadly blow has been struck at the *sovereignty of the states,* and from a quarter so far removed from the people as to be hardly accessible to public opinion—it is needless to say that we allude to the decision of the supreme court, in the case of McCulloh *versus* the state of Maryland, by which it is established that the states cannot tax the bank of the United States.

We are yet unacquainted with the grounds of this alarming decision, but of this are resolved—that nothing but the tongue of an angel can convince us of its compatibility with the constitution of the United States, in which a power to grant acts of incorporation is not delegated, and all powers not delegated are retained.

Far be it from us to be thought as speaking disrespectfully of the supreme court, or to subject ourselves to the suspicion of a "contempt" of it. We do not impute corruption to the judges, nor intimate that they have been influenced by improper feelings—they are great and learned men: *but still, only men.* And, feeling as we do— as if the very stones would cry out if we did not speak on this subject, we will exercise our right to do it—and declare, that if the supreme court is not mistaken in its construction of the constitution of the United States, or that another definition cannot be given to it by some act of the states—their sovereignty is at the mercy of their creature—congress. . . .

Where are these things to end, and what will be the consequences of them? Every person must see in them a total prostration of the state rights, and the loss of the liberties of the nation, unless the decision turns upon some *point of common* (*not* CONSTITUTIONAL) law, in the special case that has been before the supreme court. . . .

We are awfully impressed with a conviction that the welfare of the union has received a more dangerous wound than fifty *Hartford* conventions, hateful as that assemblage was, could inflict—reaching so close to the *vitals* as seemingly to draw the heart's blood of liberty and safety, and which may be wielded to destroy the *whole revenues,* and so do away the sovereignties of the states. In the progress of this principle, we can easily anticipate the time when some daring scoundrel, having fortified himself by *soul-trading incorporations,* may seize upon these fair countries for a kingdom, and, surrounded with obedient judges and lying priests, punish his opponents, after the manner of European despots, with fines, imprisonment and tortures here, and the terrors of the *lower world* hereafter. But we will not *despair of the republic,* nor yet *give up the ship;* no alternative, however, is left to preserve the sovereignty of the states but by amending the constitution of the United States, and more clearly defining the *original* intentions of that instrument in several respects, but especially in regard to *incorporations:*—these are evidences of sovereignty; congress has not a sovereign power, except in the cases *specially delegated.*

We repeat it—it is not on account of the bank of the United States that we are thus moved. Our sentiments are on record, that we did not wish the *destruction* of that institution; but, fearing the enormous power of the corporation, we were zealous that an authority to arrest its deleterious influence might be vested in *responsible* hands, *for it has not got any soul.* Yet this solitary institution may not subvert the liberties of our country, and command every one to bow down to it as *Baal;* it is the *principle* of it that alarms us, as operating against the unresigned rights of the states.

SPENCER ROANE [6]

Virginia Judge Spencer Roane offered the most important public criticism of the Marshall Court's decisions. In a series of essays in 1819, he attacked the McCulloch decision; in another group of essays in 1821, he condemned the broad, nationalistic thrust of Cohens v. Virginia. Roane published the latter in the Richmond Enquirer *under the pseudonym of Algernon Sidney. Roane's commentaries evoked favorable reaction from Jefferson and Madison, although Madison did not share Jefferson's personal antipathy toward Marshall.*

I beg leave to address you, fellow-citizens, on the subject of the late decision of the Supreme Court, in the case of *Cohens* against the *State of Virginia.* I address you on that great subject, from no light motives whatsover. Far less have I any vain desire, to array myself against the very able penman, by whom that opinion was composed. I approach you, on the contrary, with a heavy heart. I address you under a solemn conviction, that the liberties and constitution of our country are endangered—deeply and vitally endangered, by the fatal effects of that decision. . . .

My appeal to you, I trust, will not be made in vain. You are the same American people, who, twenty years ago, put down an infamous sedition-law, by the mere force of public opinion. Yes! and you also put down, therewith, the equally infamous judgments of the federal courts, by which that statute was enforced. You put down, with indignation, and with scorn, those unjust judgments, which had fined and imprisoned divers of our citizens for exercising the sacred rights of speaking and writing, guaranteed to them by the constitu-

[6] *John P. Branch Historical Papers* (Ashland, Va., 1906), 2: 78–89.

tion. Where is now that act and where are now those judgments? Crucified, dead and buried. They have descended together, to the tomb of the Capulets, and peace be to their names. . . .

The judgment now before us . . . completely negatives the idea, that the American States have a real existence, or are to be considered, in any sense, as sovereign and independent States. It does this by claiming a right to reverse the decisions of the highest judicial tribunals of those states. That state is a non-entity, as a sovereign power, the decisions of whose courts are subjected to such a revision. It is an anomaly in the science of government, that the courts of one independent government, are to control and reverse the judgments of the courts of another. The barriers and boundaries between the powers of two sovereign and independent governments, are so high and so strong, as to defy the jurisdiction, justly claimed by a superior court, over the judgments of such as are inferior. This decision also reprobates the idea that our system of government is a confederation of free states. That is no federal republic, in which one of the parties to the compact, claims the exclusive right to pass finally upon the chartered rights of another. In such a government there is no common arbiter of their rights but the people. If this power of decision is once conceded to either party, the equilibrium established by the constitution is destroyed, and the compact exists thereafter, but in name. This decision also claims the right, to amend the federal constitution, at the mere will and pleasure of the supreme court. The constitution is not the less changed or amended because it is done by construction, and in the form of a decree or judgment. In point of substance, its effect is the same; and this construction becomes a part of the constitution or of the fundamental laws. It becomes so, because it is not in the power of the ordinary legislature to alter or repeal it. This construction defies all power, but that of the people, in their primary and original character, although, in effect, it entirely changes the nature of our government. This assumption of power is the less excusible, too, fellow-citizens, because no government under Heaven, has provided so amply as ours, for necessary amendments of the constitution, by the legitimate power of the people. This decision also touches the sovereignty of the states, in another very tender point. It nullifies a statute made by one of them, to promote the morality of her people. It does this at the instance of the petty corporation of the city of Washington, and the statute of Virginia is made to yield, to an ordinance of the

Common Hall of that city. It is so made to yield by means of the most remote and unwarrantable implication. This decision does not admit the competency of the courts of the states, to enforce their own penal-laws, against their own offending citizens. It does not admit them to be impartial, in deciding the controversies of the states, with their own citizens. Nor does it allow them to enforce an act, made to promote the morality of their people. Few measures are more promotive of that end, than the abolition of gambling— and that cannot be prohibited but by penalties, like the one in question. This decision also claims the right, to bring the state government before the courts, without their consent, and without, consequently, having the necessary parties. It claims to do this, in all cases whatsoever: or which is nearly the same thing, in all cases in which the constitution, laws, and treaties of the United States may come in question. It claims that right also, at the suit of a citizen of that state: a right utterly disclaimed by our conventions, and primiaeval legislatures. It claims this right in the teeth of the eleventh amendment to the constitution, and of the enumeration contained in the third article of the original constitution, which specified the cases in which the states consented to be sued, in the federal court, and in which specification, the present case is not included. It claims it, also, in defiance of the tenth amendment to the constitution, which provides, that powers not delegated to the United States by the constitution, shall be deemed to be reserved to the several states. To "cap the climax" of this absurd picture, the court has sanctioned the right of the legislature of the district of Columbia, to act by deputy; and has exalted to the dignity of a statute of the United States an ordinance of the Common Hall of the city of Washington. It has given a force to that ordinance in every State in the Union, which is to supercede and repeal their most undoubted and salutary laws: a power, which a statute of the Congress of the United States has not, which the acts of no State in the Union have; and which is not reciprocal in favor of Virginia, either within the territory of this favored district, or that of any other State in the Union.

This most monstrous and unexampled decision, is without the apologies which may be offered for the judgments of which I have spoken. The judgments upon the sedition law, might, in some degree, be paliated, by being bottomed upon an act of the federal legislature; as that in the case of ship-money, was expressly predicated upon the supposed necessities of the kingdom. But the decision before us, finds no support from any statute; and is adopted in the most prosperous epoch of our existence, as a nation. It professes to give a true exposition of the constitution, and does not deign to seek a shelter under the pressure of any circumstances. It can only be accounted for, from that love of power, which all history informs us infects and corrupts all who possess it, and from which even the high and ermined judges, themselves, are not exempted.

It is of no account, that the judgment in question was rendered for the state of Virginia. That great and opulent state is, indeed, permitted to retain the paltry sum of one hundred dollars; but the permission is only grounded, if I may so say, upon the defectiveness of the pleadings. Whenever the actual provisions of an act of Congress, and of the ordinance consequent thereon, shall show an intention that they should operate within the territories of the states, a different decision would be given. In that case, the supremacy of such act or ordinance, would be asserted, and the most salutary indubitable provisions of the laws of the states must succomb. It is impossible that the people of any state can be thus gulled, by any decision. The case is, most emphatically, decided against them. It is so decided on grounds and principles which go the full length of destroying the state governments altogether and establishing on their ruins, one great, national, and consolidated government.

Before I go into this subject more particularly, I must be permitted again to remark upon the pretentions—allow me to say the extravagant pretensions,—of those, by whom the judgment before us has been rendered. While in other countries the judiciary has been said to be the weakest of the several departments of government, and has been limited to the mere decision of the causes brought before it, ours has aspired to a far more elevated function. It has claimed the right not only to control the operations of the co-ordinate department of its own government, but also, to settle, exclusively, as aforesaid, the chartered rights of the other parties to the compact. Being one, only, of the departments of the general government, it has claimed and exercised a right, not possessed by them all—that of judging, definitely, in its own cause, in the case of powers contested between the parties to the compact. It has claimed the right to destroy the compact, by which the states are confederated together, by construing that compact to be, whatever it pleases to make it. In a government admitted to be defective, all its defects are cured by applying the rule of *precrustes,* or are amended by the construing power of the supreme court; a power, which is equally unnecessary under the actual provisions of the constitution on that subject and dangerous, as it knows no limit but the arbitrary discretion of the judges. While that high court will scarcely allow that any other government, or any other department of its own government can do right, it acts upon the principle, that itself is never in the wrong. While it is profuse as we shall see in ascribing the most unworthy motives, to other governments, and other departments, it arrogates to itself a degree of purity scarcely equalled by the white ermine with which it is invested. It challenges a degree of infallibility scarcely claimed by the arrogant pretentions of the former Popes of Rome. There is but one higher grade in this climax of arrogance and absurdity, and that is, to claim to hold its powers by divine authority, and in utter contempt of the sovereign power of the people.

With respect to oppressions of violations of the constitution, committed by the other departments of the government, they can easily be corrected, by the elective franchise; and that franchise will be graduated, by the degree of oppression which is inflicted. But the court in question claims to hold its authority paramount to the power of the people. It is not elected by, nor is amenable to them. Having been appointed in one generation, it claims to make laws and constitutions for another. It acts always upon the foundation of its own precedents, and progresses, "with a noiseless foot and unalarming advance," until it reaches the zenith of despotic power.

The supreme court seem to have entirely forgotten, that the American people are a people jealous of their rights and priveleges. Having passed through the Red-Sea of the revolution, and foiled a formidable tyrant in the conflict, the inestimable jewel then acquired, is not to be lightly cast away. They seem to have forgotton what all history teaches us, that power is an encroaching thing, and that all men who possess it, will "feel it, and forget right." They seem to have forgotton that liberty can only be preserved by frequent elections as to two of the departments of government, and by checks and limitations judiciously applied, to the third. They seem to have claimed an exemption from the restrictions of the constitution, by the unlimited right they have usurped, to alter the constitution as they please. American history will teach that high court, on almost every page, that our people have, in all vicissitudes and changes, stickled for the division and limitation of powers. They have retained, entirely to themselves many important powers, and have refused to delegate them to any government. The powers actually delegated, have been also divided between two governments, and again sub-divided between the different departments of each government. This division and limitation of the granted powers, and the checks necessarily resulting therefrom, forms the only security of our liberties. Without these checks the balance of power would always incline in favor of the strongest government, or the strongest department of each government. But for the purpose of establishing these checks, this limitation and division of power, would have been wholly unnecessary.

The supreme court, while it must admit, that both itself and its co-ordinate departments, are to be checked by each other, (and instances of which, I shall hereafter specify) denies that any check exists, in favor of the state governments. The inference would seem to hold, a *fortiori*, in favor of the latter. It would seem to be a much smaller abuse, of the federal constitution, that a power should be exercised by one department of the same government, which was confided to another, than that one government should usurp the just powers reserved to another. If the line of demarcation between the different departments of the same government, cannot be obliterated by implication or construction, neither can that broader and bolder line, which is established between the different governments. It would be a much greater calamity to the American people, to wipe out these broader lines between the two governments, and thus establish one great consolidated government, than, by obliterating the fainter lines drawn between the different departments, to vest all the proper powers of the general government in one department. In that case they would be still federal powers, which would be exercised: but the calamity would be inconceivable, of submitting the local and municipal concern of one section of this vast country to members coming from another, and who have no common interest with them in relation thereto.

The supreme court ought not to have forgotten, that although our general government is a national one as to some purposes, it is a federal one as to others. They ought also to have remembered, that states giving up some of their rights, and becoming members of a federal republic, do not, thereby, cease to be sovereign states.

If the sovereignty of states is to be tested by the portion of power reserved, or given up, that criterion would clearly incline in favor of the state. We are told in The Federalist that the powers delegated to the general government, are "few and defined, and relate chiefly to external subjects, while the states retain a residuary and inviolable sovereignty over all other subjects; over all these great subjects, which immediately concern the prosperity of the people." Neither can that result be varied by adverting to the relative sizes, of the territories of the contracting governments. A criterion of that kind would exclude the little state of Delaware, from her equal sovereign rights under the confederation, with the great state of New York. If these facts are borne in mind, and if it is at the same time remembered, that neither the general government has received, nor the state governments have parted with, any powers but those which have been "delegated," it will be difficult to sustain the decision of the supreme court. That decision has proceeded upon the idea, that *quoad* the judicial power, the state governments are not to be respected, and the supreme courts of the several states are to be regarded as inferior federal tribunals. In relation to the judicial power, at least, the states are not admitted to be sovereign.

These, fellow-citizens, are some of the objections I have to make to the decision of the Supreme Court. I shall, probably, advert to many others in the progress of my observations upon it. It is my purpose to endeavor to examine that decision under all its objectionable aspects and bearings. It is no small proof of the badness of the cause, espoused by that decision, that the opinion before us is objectionable, not only in its principles, but, also, in its form and structure. Considering the great talents by which it was composed, this defect cannot be otherwise accounted for. The opinion, besides being unusually tedious, and tautologous abounds in defects which are more important. It often adopts premises which cannot be conceded, and takes for granted, the very points which are to be proved. Its slips in history and in facts are but few and its sophistries are glaring and innumerable. If my remarks are tedious, tautologous, and desultory, it is because the opinion, in itself, is so. . . .

WILLIAM LEGGETT

Marshall's death in 1835 evoked an outburst of adulation that sometimes bordered on the fulsome. One exception, how-

*ever, was the following editorial written by William Leggett
in the* New York Evening Post. *Exhibiting a candor all too
uncommon for such editorials, Leggett, a Jacksonian Democrat,
reminded his readers of Marshall's political antecedents and
principles—ones, of course, decidedly out of favor in the Age
of Jackson.* Niles' Register *reprinted Leggett's editorial and
commented it was the only "thing of the sort" that appeared
at the time.*[7]

Judge Marshall was a man of very considerable talents and
acquirements, and great amiableness of private character. His political doctrines, unfortunately, were of the ultra federal or aristo-
cratic kind. He was one of those who, with Hamilton, distrusted
the virtue and intelligence of the people, and was in favor of a
strong and vigorous general government, at the expense of the rights
of the states and of the people. His judicial decisions of all questions
involving political principles have been uniformly on the side of
implied powers and a free construction of the constitution, and such
also has been the uniform tendency of his writings. That he was
sincere in these views, we do not express a doubt, nor that he truly
loved his country; but that he has been all his life long, a stumbling
block and impediment in the way of democratic principles no one
can deny, and his situation, therefore, at the head of an important
tribunal, constituted in utter defiance of the very first principles of
democracy, has always been to us, as we have before frankly stated,
an occasion of lively regret. *That he is at length removed from that
station* IS A SOURCE OF SATISFACTION, while at the same time
we trust we entertain a proper sentiment for the death of a good
and exemplary man.

[7] *New York Evening Post,* July 10, 1835.

7

In Praise

JOHN ADAMS [1]

Certainly, John Adams appointed Marshall chief justice for a variety of motives—to retaliate against Hamilton and the extreme Federalists, to reward the Virginian's loyalty to a lameduck, isolated president, or, just possibly, because he admired and respected Marshall's political and constitutional views and considered him eminently fit for the position. In any event, his appointment of Marshall ultimately proved to be one of the most significant acts of Adams's presidency, a fact that the ex-president acknowledged in the twilight of his life.

There is no part of my life that I look back upon with more pleasure, than the short time I spent with you. And it is the pride of my life that I have given to this nation a Chief Justice equal to Coke or Hale, Holt or Mansfield.

I am unalterably your friend, and well wisher though on the point of departure.

JOHN QUINCY ADAMS [2]

John Quincy Adams viewed Marshall's career from a variety of perspectives—as congressman, cabinet officer, and president. He regarded his father's appointment of Marshall as one of the "most important" acts of his administration. Writing in his diary after the chief justice's death, the younger Adams set the tone for future historians who tried to summarize Marshall's work as essentially a counterpoise to the destructive tendencies of Jeffersonian democracy. Adams's thoughts in

[1] Adams to Marshall, August 17, 1825, Gray–Elines Collection, Connecticut State Library.

[2] Charles Francis Adams, ed., *Memoirs of John Quincy Adams,* vol. 9 (Philadelphia, 1876), entries of July 10, August 10, 1835, 9: 243–44, 251.

*1835 typically reflected the despair of Andrew Jackson's ene-
mies and of those who feared that the loss of Marshall would
further impair national power.*

John Marshall . . . was one of the most eminent men that
this country has ever produced. He has held this appointment thirty-
five years. It was the last act of my father's Administration, and one
of the most important services rendered by him to his country. All
constitutional governments are flexible things; and as the Supreme
Judicial Court is the tribunal of last resort for the construction of
the Constitution and the laws, the office of Chief Justice of that
Court is a station of the highest trust, of the deepest responsibility,
and of influence far more extensive than that of the President of
the United States. John Marshall was a federalist of the Washington
school. The Associate Judges from the time of his appointment have
generally been taken from the Democratic, or Jeffersonian party.
Not one of them, excepting Story, has been a man of great ability.
Several of them have been men of strong prejudices, warm passions,
and contracted minds; one of them, occasionally insane. Marshall,
by the ascendency of his genius, by the amenity of his deportment,
and by the imperturbable command of his temper, has given a permanent and systematic character to the decisions of the Court, and
settled many great constitutional questions favorably to the continuance of the Union. Marshall has cemented the Union which
the crafty and quixotic democracy of Jefferson had a perpetual
tendency to dissolve. Jefferson hated and dreaded him. Marshall
kept Jefferson much under the curb—sometimes, as perhaps in the
case of Aaron Burr's conspiracy, too much so; but Marshall's mind
was far better regulated than that of Jefferson. It is much to be
feared that a successor will be appointed of a very different character. The President of the United States now in office has already
appointed three Judges of the Supreme Court; with the next appointment he will have constituted the Chief Justice and a majority
of the Court. He has not yet made one good appointment. His Chief
Justice will be no better than the rest. . . .

The office of Chief Justice of the Supreme Court is held for life,
that of the President of the United States only for four, or at most
for eight, years. The office of Chief Justice requires a mind of energy

sufficient to influence generally the minds of a majority of his associates; to accommodate his judgment to theirs, or theirs to his own; a judgment also capable of abiding the test of time and of giving satisfaction to the public. It requires a man profoundly learned in the law of nations, in the commercial and maritime law, in the civil law, in the common law of England, and in the general statute laws of the several States of the Union. With all these powers steadily exercised during a period of thirty-four years, Chief-Justice Marshall has settled many questions of constitutional law, certainly more than all the Presidents of the United States together.

PHILIP HONE [3]

Philip Hone, businessman and former mayor of New York City, expressed sentiments similar to John Quincy Adams's, particularly in his concern for Marshall's successor. Andrew Jackson's nomination of Roger B. Taney confirmed Hone's worst fears.

JULY 1. . . . I know of no greater misfortune which our country could sustain at this time than the death of Chief Justice Marshall. He is the sheet-anchor of the Constitution; pure, enlightened, and patriotic; the loss of such a man would be a national calamity at any time, but it is a fearful thing to think of his place being filled by a man who is willing to sacrifice everything we hold sacred to the gratification of his personal feelings and the aggrandizement of his party. . . .

JULY 8. . . . The calamity which has for some time past threatened our country has happened at last, and every man who admires talents and venerates virtue mourns over the loss we have sustained. John Marshall, the wise, the virtuous, the patriotic, died on the afternoon of Monday the 6th inst., at six o'clock, in Philadelphia, in which city he has been for some time, to avail himself of the best medical advice. Take the Chief Justice for all in all, he combined in his character more good and great qualities than any other man in the United States during his or any other time, with the

[3] Bayard Tuckerman, ed., *Diary of Philip Hone, 1828–1851*, 2 vols. (New York, 1889), entries of July 1, 8, 10, 18, 1835, 1: 145–49.

exception of his friend and associate, Washington; and his death at this time is a greater national calamity than Washington's was when it occurred. . . . Would it had pleased Divine Providence to delay the stroke for a few years! Less danger would be apprehended if the successor of General Jackson had had the filling of this most important office, even if that successor were (as it most probably will be) Mr. Van Buren. He will be governed less by personal predilections, and if he has no more virtue than the present incumbent, he has more policy and less reliance upon his own infallibility. At any rate, I would rather trust him.

In 1797 Marshall was appointed by President Adams, with General Pinckney and Elbridge Gerry, to negotiate with the French Directory. They were not received by the French, and it was in this embassy that the famous X. Y. Z. correspondence was instituted, in which the envoys were invited to bribe the Directory as the means of obtaining justice for this country. It was this infamous proposal which gave rise to the celebrated expression so frequently quoted, "Millions for defence, not a cent for tribute." In 1799 he was elected and took his seat in Congress. Here his talents became immediately so conspicious that in 1800 he was appointed Secretary of War, and on the 31st of January, 1801, he became Chief Justice of the Supreme Court of the United States, which distinguished position he continued to fill with unsullied dignity and preëminent ability until the close of his mortal career. All newspapers are, as they ought to be, clad in mourning.

JULY 10.—Charles King gave me, on board the steamboat, yesterday morning the "Evening Post" to read an infamous editorial notice of the death of Chief Justice Marshall. They say he was a man of *considerable talents!* but an enemy to Democratic principles, and used his influence in the court over which he presided to subvert them, and on the whole his removal is a cause of rejoicing. This is absolutely a species of impiety for which I want words to express my abhorrence. It is of a piece with Duane's celebrated article published in the "Aurora" on the death of Washington, beginning with the scriptural quotation, "Lord, now lettest thou thy servant depart in peace, for mine eyes have seen thy salvation;" and the painful recollection of these two great national bereavements will ever be accompanied in the minds of all good Americans by their detestation of the sentiments of the two compeers in infamy, who have thus acquired a most unenviable notoriety. The "Times," another of our Jackson papers, on the other hand, has noticed the Chief Justice's death in the most feeling manner, and consecrated his memory by eulogiums which none but a fool would deny, or a knave withhold.

JULY 18.—The papers contain a report that the President has appointed Roger B. Taney Chief Justice of the United States in the place of the lamented John Marshall. Mr. Taney is a lawyer of high reputation, and except in his slavish devotion to General Jackson and his party, which led him during his short career as Secretary of the Treasury to perform an act of subserviency which must "damn him to everlasting fame," he was always esteemed a respectable man. The act alluded to, the acceptance of office solely to do the President's dirty work of removing the deposits, was sufficient to entitle him to this or any other office in his gift; and as none but a person possessing that sort of qualification would be appointed, it is fortunate, on the whole, that the ermine has not fallen upon less worthy shoulders. If this appointment has been made, and Mr. Van Buren should be elected President (of which I think there is very little doubt), the remarkable fact will be disclosed of the two most exalted offices in the country being held by individuals whose nominations for other offices of greatly inferior importance have been rejected by the Senate.

JOSEPH STORY [4]

Marshall had close relations with most of his colleagues, but he was most intimate with Joseph Story. Although Story had been appointed to the high bench in 1811 as a Jeffersonian Republican, he and Marshall shared the same legal and constitutional outlook. Story's adulation of Marshall often bordered on the religious; the following discourse on the chief justice's career vividly reflects the younger man's admiration and devotion. After Marshall's death, Story was inconsolable and seriously considered resigning from the Court. Nevertheless, he stayed on, often dissenting from the views of the new majority, which he regarded as dangerous deviations from the wisdom laid down during the Marshall years. He often de-

[4] Joseph Story, *A Discourse upon the Life, Character, and Services of the Honorable John Marshall* . . . (Boston, 1835), pp. 5, 49–50, 56–60, 64–65, 70–73.

scribed himself as the "last of the old race of judges"; indeed,
he spent the last decade of his judicial career largely in philo-
sophical and political isolation from his colleagues.

. . . The life of Chief Justice Marshall, though unadorned by
brilliant passages of individual adventure, or striking events, carries
with it, (unless I am greatly mistaken,) that, which is the truest
title to renown, a fame founded on public and private virtue. It has
happened to him, as to many other distinguished men, that his life
had few incidents; and those, which belonged to it, were not far
removed from the ordinary course of human events. That life was
filled up in the conscientious discharge of duty. It was throughout
marked by a wise and considerate propriety. His virtues expanded
with the gradual development of his character. They were the natural growth of deep rooted principles, working their way through
the gentlest affections, and the purest ambition. No man ever had
a loftier desire of excellence; but it was tempered by a kindness,
which subdued envy, and a diffidence, which extinguished jealousy.
Search his whole life, and you cannot lay your finger on a single
extravagance of design or act. There were no infirmities, leaving a
permanent stain behind them. There were no eccentricities to be
concealed; no follies to be apologized for; no vices to be blushed
at; no rash outbreakings of passionate resentment to be regretted;
no dark deeds, disturbing the peace of families, or leaving them
wretched by its desolations. If here and there the severest scrutiny
might be thought capable of detecting any slight admixture of human frailty, it was so shaded off in its coloring, that it melted into
some kindred virtue. . . .
There was throughout his political life a steadfastness and consistency of principle as striking, as they were elevating. During more
than half a century of public service, he maintained with inflexible
integrity the same political principles, with which he begun. He
was content to live *by, with,* and *for* his principles. Amidst the ex-
travagancies of parties at different times, he kept on the even tenor
of his way with a calm and undeviating firmness, never bending
under the pressure of adversity, or bounding with the elasticity of
success. His counsels were always the counsels of moderation, fortified and tried by the results of an enlightened experience. They
never betrayed either timidity or rashness. He was, in the original,

genuine sense of the word, a Federalist—a Federalist of the good old school, of which Washington was the acknowledged head, and in which he lived and died. In the maintenance of the principles of that school he was ready at all times to stand forth a determined advocate and supporter. On this subject he scorned all disguise; he affected no change of opinion; he sought no shelter from reproach. He boldly, frankly, and honestly avowed himself, through evil report and good report, the disciple, the friend, and the admirer of Washington and his political principles. He had lived in times, when these principles seemed destined to secure to the party, to which he belonged, an enduring triumph. He had lived to see all these prospects blasted; and other statesmen succeed with a power and influence of such vast extent, that it extinguished all hopes of any future return to office. Yet he remained unshaken, unseduced, unterrified. He had lived to see many of his old friends pass on the other side; and the gallant band, with which he had borne the strife, drop away by death, one after another, until it seemed reduced to a handful. Yet he uttered neither a sigh, nor a complaint. When, under extraordinary excitements in critical times, others, with whom he had acted, despaired of the Republic, and were willing to yield it up to a stern necessity, he resisted the impulse, and clung to the Union, and nailed its colors to the mast of the Constitution.

It is no part of my duty or design upon the present occasion to expound, or vindicate his political opinions. That would of itself furnish ample materials for a discourse of a different character. But it is due to truth to declare, that no man was ever more sincerely attached to the principles of free government; no man ever cherished republican institutions with more singleness of heart and purpose; no man ever adhered to his country with a stronger filial affection; no man in his habits, manners, feelings, pursuits, and actions, ever exemplified more perfectly that idol of chivalry, a patriot without fear and without reproach. But, on the other hand, no man was ever more sensible of the dangers incident to free institutions, and especially of those, which threaten our national existence. He saw and felt, where the weaknesses of the Republic lay. He wished, earnestly wished, perpetuity to the Constitution, as the only solid foundation of our national glory and independence. But he foresaw what our course would be; and he never hesitated to express, what his fears were, and whence the ruin of the Constitution must come, if it shall come at all. In his view, the Republic is not destined to perish, if it shall perish, by the overwhelming power of the National Government; but by the resisting and counteracting power of the State sovereignties. He thought with another kindred mind, whose vivid language still rings in my ears after many years, as a voice from the dead, that in our Government the centrifugal force is far greater than the centripetal; that the danger is not, that we shall fall into the sun; but that we may fly off in eccentric orbits, and never return to our perihelion. Whether his prophetic fears were ill or well founded, Time alone can decide;— Time, which sweeps away the schemes of man's invention; but leaves immovable on their foundations the eternal truths of nature. . . .

He was a great man. I do not mean by this, that among his contemporaries he was justly entitled to a high rank for his intellectual endowments, an equal among the master spirits of the day, if not *facile princeps*. I go farther; and insist, that he would have been deemed a great man in any age, and of all ages. He was one of those, to whom centuries alone give birth; standing out, like beacon lights on the loftiest eminences, to guide, admonish, and instruct future generations, as well as the present. It did not happen to him, as it has happened to many men of celebrity, that he appeared greatest at a distance; that his superiority vanished on a close survey; and that familiarity brought it down to the standard of common minds. On the contrary, it required some degree of intimacy fully to appreciate his powers; and those, who knew him best, and saw him most, had daily reason to wonder at the vast extent and variety of his intellectual resources.

His genius was rather contemplative, than imaginative. It seemed not so much to give direction to his other intellectual powers, as to receive its lead from them. He devoted himself principally to serious and profound studies; and employed his invention rather to assist philosophical analysis, than to gather materials for ornament, for persuasion, or for picturesque effect. In strength, and depth, and comprehensiveness of mind, it would be difficult to name his superior. . . .

But it is principally upon his character as a Magistrate, presiding over the highest tribunal of the Nation, that the solid fabric of his fame must rest. And there let it rest; for the foundations are deep, and the superstructure fitted for immortality. Time, which is perpetually hurrying into a common oblivion the flatterers of kings, and the flatterers of the people, the selfish demagogues, and the wary courtiers, serves but to make true greatness better known, by dissolving the mists of prejudice and passion, which for a while conceal its true glory. The life of the Chief Justice extended over a space rare in the annals of jurisprudence; and still more rare is such a life, with the accompaniment of increasing reputation. There was nothing accidental or adventitious in his judicial character. It grew by its own native strength, unaided by the sunshine of power, and unchecked by cold neglect, or unsparing indifference. . . .

. . . his peculiar triumph was in the exposition of constitutional law. It was here, that he stood confessedly without a rival, whether we regard his thorough knowledge of our civil and political history, his admirable powers of illustration and generalization, his scrupulous integrity and exactness in interpretation, or his consummate skill in moulding his own genius into its elements, as if they had constituted the exclusive study of his life. His proudest epitaph may be written in a single line—Here lies the Expounder of the Constitution of the United States. . . .

Let it be remembered, that, when Chief Justice Marshall first took his seat on the Bench, scarcely more than two or three questions of constitutional law had ever engaged the attention of the Supreme Court. As a science, constitutional law was then confessedly new; and that portion of it, in an especial manner, which may be subjected to judicial scrutiny, had been explored by few minds, even in the most general forms of inquiry. Let it be remembered, that in the course of his judicial life, numerous questions of a practical nature, and involving interests of vast magnitude, have been constantly before the Court, where there was neither guide, nor authority; but all was to be wrought out by general principles. Let it be remembered, that texts, which scarcely cover the breadth of a finger, have been since interpreted, explained, limited, and adjusted by judicial commentaries, which are now expanded into volumes. Let it be remembered, that the highest learning, genius, and eloquence of the bar, have been employed to raise doubts, and fortify objections; that State sovereignties have stood impeached in their legislation; and rights of the most momentous nature have been suspended upon the issue; that, under such circumstances, the infirmities of false reasoning, the glosses of popular appeal, the scattered fire of irregular and inconclusive assertion, and the want of comprehensive powers of analysis, had no chance to escape the instant detection of the profession;—Let these things (I say) be remembered; and who does not at once perceive, that the task of expounding the Constitution, under such circumstances, required almost superhuman abilities? It demanded a mind, in which vast reaches of thought should be combined with patience of investigation, sobriety of judgment, fearlessness of consequences, and mastery of the principles of interpretation, to an extent rarely belonging to the most gifted of our race.

How this gigantic task of expounding the Constitution was met and executed by Chief Justice Marshall, let the Profession, let the Public, decide. Situated as I am, I may not speak for others upon such an occasion. But having sat by his side during twenty-four years; having witnessed his various constitutional labors; having heard many of those exquisite judgments, the fruits of his own unassisted meditations, from which the Court has derived so much honor;—*et nos aliquod nomenque decusque gessimus;*—I confess myself unable to find language sufficiently expressive of my admiration and reverence of his transcendent genius. . . . The praise is sincere, though it may be perishable. Not so his fame. It will flow on to the most distant ages. Even if the Constitution of his country should perish, his glorious judgments will still remain to instruct mankind, until liberty shall cease to be a blessing, and the science of jurisprudence shall vanish from the catalogue of human pursuits.

PART THREE

JOHN MARSHALL IN HISTORY

8

Oliver Wendell Holmes

Holmes's estimate of Marshall was delivered (in response to a motion for adjournment of the Massachusetts Supreme Judicial Court) to honor the one hundredth anniversary of Marshall's assumption of the chief justiceship. Hundreds of speeches and memorials were given throughout the nation on that day, but only Holmes's is memorable. It is a typical Holmesian statement—pithy, skeptical, and metaphorical. Perhaps somewhat extreme in his deprecation of Marshall's role, this judgment nevertheless serves as a counterpoint to the typical adulation of Marshall in Holmes's day. Moreover, it offers a useful beginning for a serious critical evaluation of Marshall's contributions.[1]

If I were to think of John Marshall simply by number and measure in the abstract, I might hesitate in my superlatives, just as I should hesitate over the battle of the Brandywine if I thought of it apart from its place in the line of historic cause. But such thinking is empty in the same proportion that it is abstract. It is most idle to take a man apart from the circumstances which, in fact, were his. To be sure, it is easier in fancy to separate a person from his riches than from his character. But it is just as futile. Remove a square inch of mucous membrane, and the tenor will sing no more. Remove a little cube from the brain, and the orator will be speechless; or another, and the brave, generous and profound spirit becomes a timid and querulous trifler. A great man represents a

---

[1] John F. Dillon, ed., *John Marshall: Life, Character and Judicial Services as Portrayed in . . . Addresses and Proceedings . . . on Marshall Day, 1901 . . . ,* 3 vols. (Chicago, 1903), 1: 204–208.

great ganglion in the nerves of society, or, to vary the figure, a strategic point in the campaign of history, and part of his greatness consists in his being *there*. I no more can separate John Marshall from the fortunate circumstance that the appointment of Chief Justice fell to John Adams, instead of to Jefferson a month later, and so gave it to a Federalist and loose constructionist to start the working of the Constitution, than I can separate the black line through which he sent his electric fire at Fort Wagner from Colonel Shaw. When we celebrate Marshall we celebrate at the same time and indivisibly the inevitable fact that the oneness of the nation and the supremacy of the national Constitution were declared to govern the dealings of man with man by the judgments and decrees of the most august of courts.

I do not mean, of course, that personal estimates are useless or teach us nothing. No doubt to-day there will be heard from able and competent persons such estimates of Marshall. But I will not trench upon their field of work. It would be out of place when I am called on only to express the answer to a motion addressed to the court and when many of those who are here are to listen this afternoon to the accomplished teacher who has had every occasion to make a personal study of the judge, and again this evening to a gentleman who shares by birth the traditions of the man. My own impressions are only those that I have gathered in the common course of legal education and practice. In them I am conscious, perhaps, of some little revolt from our purely local or national estimates, and of a wish to see things and people judged by more cosmopolitan standards. A man is bound to be parochial in his practice—to give his life, and if necessary his death, for the place where he has his roots. But his thinking should be cosmopolitan and detached. He should be able to criticise what he reveres and loves.

The Federalist, when I read it many years ago, seemed to me a truly original and wonderful production for the time. I do not trust even that judgment unrevised when I remember that *The Federalist* and its authors struck a distinguished English friend of mine as finite; and I should feel a greater doubt whether, after Hamilton and the Constitution itself, Marshall's work proved more than a strong intellect, a good style, personal ascendancy in his court, courage, justice and the convictions of his party. My keenest interest is excited, not by what are called great questions and great cases, but by little decisions which the common run of selectors would pass by because they did not deal with the Constitution or a telephone company, yet which have in them the germ of some wider theory, and therefore of some profound interstitial change in the very tissue of the law. The men whom I should be tempted to commemorate would be the originators of transforming thought. They often are half obscure, because what the world pays for is judgment, not the original mind.

But what I have said does not mean that I shall join in this celebration or in granting the motion before the court in any half-hearted way. Not only do I recur to what I said in the beginning, and remembering that you cannot separate a man from his place, remember also that there fell to Marshall perhaps the greatest place that ever was filled by a judge; but when I consider his might, his justice, and his wisdom, I do fully believe that if American law were to be represented by a single figure, sceptic and worshipper alike would agree without dispute that the figure could be one alone, and that one, John Marshall.

A few words more and I have done. We live by symbols, and what shall be symbolized by any image of the sight depends upon the mind of him who sees it. The setting aside of this day in honor of a great judge may stand to a Virginian for the glory of his glorious State; to a patriot for the fact that time has been on Marshall's side, and that the theory for which Hamilton argued, and he decided, and Webster spoke, and Grant fought, and Lincoln died, is now our corner-stone. To the more abstract but farther-reaching contemplation of the lawyer, it stands for the rise of a new body of jurisprudence, by which guiding principles are raised above the reach of statute and State, and judges are entrusted with a solemn and hitherto unheard-of authority and duty. To one who lives in what may seem to him a solitude of thought, this day—as it marks the triumph of a man whom some Presidents of his time bade carry out his judgments as he could—this day marks the fact that all thought is social, is on its way to action; that, to borrow the expression of a French writer, every idea tends to become first a catechism and then a code; and that according to its worth his unhelped meditation may one day mount a throne, and without armies, or even with them, may shoot across the world the electric despotism of an unresisted power. It is all a symbol, if you like, but so is the flag. The flag is but a bit of bunting to one who insists on prose. Yet, thanks to Marshall and to the men of his generation—and for this above all we celebrate him and them—its red is our lifeblood, its stars our world, its blue our heaven. It owns our land. At will it throws away our lives.

The motion of the bar is granted, and the court will now adjourn.

9

Vernon L. Parrington

*The Populist-Progressive critique of the Constitu-
tion as an economic document favoring special interests has
dominated much of American historical writing in the twen-
tieth century. In this view, the framers of the Constitution basically were nationalist, antidemocratic, and property-conscious
men who imposed a scheme of government favorable to their
interests and utterly disregarded popular attitudes and desires.
As a corollary to this, Marshall's judicial decisions often have
been interpreted as conscious efforts devoted to the class interests of a small elite. That Marshall's work served social and economic purposes is, of course, beyond question; but at the same
time, it is possible that those purposes served broad national
interests and desires. Vernon L. Parrington's multivolumed
study of American political and cultural thought included the
following classic treatment of Marshall and the "darker side"
of American history.[1]*

Unlike John Taylor of Caroline, whose fame lies buried with
his cause, the reputation of John Marshall has taken on immense
proportions with the later triumph of his principles. There is abundant reason for the veneration in which he has come to be held by
present-day disciples of Hamilton. More than any other man he
saved the future for Federalism. During the critical years of the
Jeffersonian and Jacksonian assaults upon the outworks of nationalism, he held the inner keep of the law, and prepared for the larger
victories that came long after he was in his grave. His strategic
judicial decisions served as a causeway over which passed the eighteenth-century doctrine of the sovereignty of the law, to unite with
the new philosophy of capitalistic exploitation. The turbid waters

[1] From Vernon L. Parrington, *Main Currents in American Thought*, volume
II, pp. 20–23. Copyright 1927, 1930, by Harcourt Brace Jovanovich, Inc.; renewed,
1955, 1958 by Vernon L. Parrington, Jr., Louis P. Tucker, Elizabeth P. Thomas.
Reprinted by permission of the publishers.

of frontier leveling and states-rights democracy washed fiercely about him, but he went on quietly with his self-appointed work. He was one man who would not bow his neck to the majority yoke, would not worship the democratic Baal. He profoundly distrusted the principle of confederation. Convinced that the "continental belt" must be buckled tightly, he gave unstinted service to the cause of consolidation. The imperative need of a sovereign political state to curb the disintegrating forces of America was axiomatic in his thinking. Looking upon all democratic aspirations as calculated to destroy federal sovereignty, and convinced that the principle of equalitarianism was a bow strung to wield against society, he stoutly upheld the principle of minority rule as the only practical agency of stable and orderly government. Holding such views it was a matter of high and patriotic duty with Marshall to use his official position to prevent the majority will from endangering interests which were far more sacred in his eyes than any natural rights propagated in the hothouse of French philosophy. He was the last of the old school of Federalists and the first of the new.

That John Marshall should have come out of Virginia is perhaps the most ironical fact in the political history of the Old Dominion. Quite unrepresentative of the dominant planter group that had gone over to Jefferson, bitterly hostile to the agrarian interests that spoke through John Taylor, he was the leader of a small remnant of Virginians who followed Washington through the fierce extremes of party conflict. He was the last and ablest representative of that older middle-class Virginia, given to speculation and intent on money-making, that was being superseded by a cavalier Virginia concerned about quite other things than financial interests. He belonged rather to Boston than to Richmond. His intense prejudices were primarily property prejudices. He was the Fisher Ames of the South, embodying every principle of the dogmatic tie-wig school of New England Federalists. Profoundly influenced by Hamilton and Robert Morris, he seems to have found the Boston group more congenial in temper and outlook. The explanation of his strong property-consciousness is to be discovered both in his material ambitions and his professional interests. He was a business man rather than a planter. He was heavily involved in land speculation and held stock in numerous corporations launched to exploit the resources of the state. Robert Morris, whose daughter married Marshall's younger brother, was his financial adviser and advanced money with which to purchase the Fairfax estate, an investment that cost the buyers the very considerable sum of fourteen thousand pounds and numerous lawsuits. He was a director in banks and a legal adviser in important cases involving property rights. His financial interests overran state boundaries and his political principles followed easily in their train, washing away all local and sectional loyalties.

Like his kinsman Jefferson, Marshall was bred on the Virginia frontier, and to the end of his life he retained the easy and careless democracy of dress and manners that marked his early environment. In his deportment he was far removed from the prim respectability of the Boston Federalists. A friendly, likable man, fond of pitching horsehoes and sitting in a game of cards, he was outwardly a genial member of the crude little Richmond world where politics and law and speculation engrossed the common attention. An easygoing nature, he was wholly wanting in intellectual interests. Strangely ill-read in the law, he was even more ignorant of history and economics and political theory. His mind took an early set, and hardened into rigidity during the reactionary years that lay between Shays's Rebellion and the rise of Napoleon. Of social and humanitarian interests he was utterly devoid. One might as well look for the sap of idealism in a last year's stump as in John Marshall. French romantic philosophy he regarded as the mother of all vicious leveling. There is no indication that he had ever heard of the Physiocratic school of economics, or had looked into the writings of Rousseau or Godwin or Paine. The blind sides of his mind were many; his intellectual contacts were few; yet what he saw and understood he grasped firmly. The narrowness of his outlook intensified the rigidity with which he held to his fixed opinions; and his extraordinary courage coupled with a dominant personality clothed his strategic position as Chief Justice with fateful influence on the later institutional development of America.

Although Marshall's later fame is the fame of a lawyer, he was in reality a politician whom fate in the person of John Adams placed on the Supreme Court bench at a critical moment, where his political opinions translated themselves into the organic law of the land, and shaped the constitution to special and particular ends. Masterful, tenacious, manipulating his fellow judges like putty, he was a judicial sovereign who for thirty-five years molded the plastic constitution to such form as pleased him, and when he died the work was so thoroughly done that later generations have not been able to undo it. His political opinions, therefore, become a matter of very great importance to the historian, for they help to explain the peculiar direction taken by our constitutional development. Materials for a just estimate of his remarkable career were long wanting, but with the appearance of Beveridge's able and explicit *Life of John Marshall* it is now possible to view him in exact historical perspective. Carefully documented, the work is a genial and readable interpretation that will go far to revivify the fame of the great Federalist. And yet in spite of its abundant documentation—drawn perhaps somewhat overmuch from Federalist sources—it is essentially a *biographie à thèse* that is careful to magnify the nationalism of its hero and to minify the property consciousness. It provides a picturesque setting, but it is a bit careless in its evaluation of the rival philosophies then struggling for supremacy. Concerning the economics of the great contest between Federalism and Republicanism it offers very inadequate information, with the result that Jefferson is reduced to the status of a master politician set over against the constructive statesman. The intellectual limitations of the lawyer have reacted in these pages upon his political enemy. Certain of the old Federalist prejudices have come to life again in these entertaining pages.

The two fixed conceptions which dominated Marshall throughout his long career on the bench were the sovereignty of the federal state and the sanctity of private property; and these found their justification in the virulence of his hatred of democracy. No man in America was less democratic in his political convictions. Underneath the free and easy exterior of the Chief Justice was as stalwart a reactionary as ever sat on the Supreme Court bench. He was utterly indifferent to popular views, and he calmly overturned the electoral verdicts of his fellow Americans with the deliberateness of a born autocrat. Not only were his important decisions political opinions, but they were Federalist opinions. America had made definite choice between the Federalist and Republican theories of government. It had repudiated the rule of "gentlemen of principle and property" and set up a very different rule. But to this mandate of the supposedly sovereign people Marshall declined to yield. Defeated at the polls, no longer in control of the executive and legislative branches of the government, Federalism found itself reintrenched in the prejudices of John Marshall. He boldly threw down the gage to the majority will, and when the long fierce struggle was over, he had effectively written into the fundamental law of the land the major tenets of the repudiated philosophy. "Judicial statesmanship," Mr. Beveridge calls these political decisions, and bids us admire statesmanship on the bench; yet the phrase runs so far as to merge the judge in the politician—an honest but somewhat indiscreet admission that the law may be twisted to partisan ends. The frankly political nature of Marshall's decisions was universally recognized at the time, and this explains the intense partisanship they evoked, the fury of the Republicans and the extravagant praise of the Federalists. The so-called Jeffersonian assault on the judiciary, of which so much has been made by the orthodox historians, and which came near to wrecking the system, was not primarily an attack upon the courts but upon political judges who used their places to serve party ends. It is a dangerous thing for the bench to twist the law to partisan or class purposes, yet to this very thing John Marshall was notoriously given. . . .

10
Edward S. Corwin

The distinguished constitutional historian Edward S. Corwin, like most commentators of his generation, viewed Marshall as a conservative and a nationalist. Yet as Corwin witnessed the profound changes in American governmental policies in the 1930s, he realized that Marshall's constitutional doctrines offered a convenient rationale for such change. In this selection, Corwin estimated the impact and relevance of Marshall's work a century after his death. Corwin, however, wisely avoided characterizing an eighteenth-century Federalist as a twentieth-century New Dealer. Instead, Corwin believed, Marshall proved to be a revolutionist malgré lui—a revolutionist in spite of himself.[1]

In the final chapter but one of his biography of Marshall, Beveridge characterizes the aging Marshall as "the Supreme Conservative." Yet when Marshall first emerged on the national scene it was as a revolutionist in the fullest sense, and 106 years after his death, it was Marshall's version of the Constitution which supplied the constitutional basis for the most profound revolution in the history of our constitutional law. In this paper I shall deal briefly with the intervening story—the story, to wit, of the evolution of the federal concept in the thinking of the Supreme Court. . . .

Marshall's assumption of the Chief Justiceship marks the beginning of his career as the "Supreme Conservative." Henceforth all his abilities would be directed to advancing through the Court the principles which underlay the Constitution, as he understood them, and these abilities were of a high order. Even Justice Holmes, while demurring to Senator Lodge's estimate of Marshall as "a nation-maker, a state-builder," conceded him, a bit condescendingly to be

---

[1] Excerpts from Edward S. Corwin, "John Marshall, Revolutionist *Malgré Lui*," 104 *University of Pennsylvania Law Review* 9 (1955). (Footnotes deleted.) Reprinted with permission of *University of Pennsylvania Law Review*.

sure, "a strong intellect, a good style, personal ascendancy in his court, courage, justice and the convictions of his party." Two things Holmes omitted: a profound conviction of calling and a singular ability, in the words of a contemporary, to "put his own ideas into the heads of others without their knowing it"—the residue, one may surmise, of his youthful experience as nurse-maid to a whole squadron of younger brothers and sisters.

The chief canons of Marshall's interpretation of the Constitution were the juristic weapons by which that interpretation became law of the land. For the purposes of this paper, they may be briefly summarized as follows:

1. The finality of the Court's interpretation of the law, and hence of the Constitution, which was the backbone of the doctrine of judicial review, as set forth particularly in *Marbury v. Madison* in relation to acts of Congress, and in *Cohens v. Virginia* in relation to state laws and constitutional provisions.

2. The popular origin of the Constitution, and its continuous vitality. The Constitution was "designed to endure for ages to come and hence to be adapted to the various crises of human affairs." The terms in which it grants power to the national government must, therefore, be liberally construed. The *locus classicus* of these doctrines is Marshall's decision in 1819 in *McCulloch v. Maryland*.

3. The principle of national supremacy, which amounted to neither more nor less than a literal application of article VI, paragraph 2 of the Constitution: "This Constitution and the laws of the United States which shall be made in pursuance thereof and the treaties made or which shall be made under the authority of the United States, shall be the supreme law of the land, and the judges in every State shall be bound thereby, anything in the Constitution or laws of any State to the contrary notwithstanding." This language, Marshall held, ruled out *ab initio* any idea that the coexistence of the states and their powers imposed limits on national power. The *locus classicus* of this doctrine is . . . his great opinion in *Gibbons v. Ogden,* where the scope of Congress' power to regulate commerce afforded the immediate issue. . . .

Even, however, before Marshall had ascended the bench, the groundwork had been laid for a radically different conception of the union, viz. that of a union of sovereign states, whose reserved powers, recognized in amendment X, stood on a footing of equality with the delegated powers of the general government. The first adumbration of such a conception appears in *Federalist #39,* the author of which was James Madison, and it was further elaborated and extended in the Virginia and Kentucky Resolutions of 1798 and 1799. It is hardly surprising, therefore, that as Marshall proceeded to develop his nationalizing principles, "the sleeping spirit of Virginia, if indeed it may ever be said to sleep," was aroused to protest.

Approaching Marshall's opinion in *McCulloch v. Maryland* from the angle of his quasi-parental concern for "the balance between the States and the National Government," Madison declared its central vice to be that it treated the powers of the latter as "sovereign powers," a view which must inevitably "convert a limited into an unlimited government," for, he continued, "in the great system of political economy, having for its general object the national welfare, everything is related immediately or remotely to every other thing; and, consequently, a power over any one thing, if not limited by some obvious and precise affinity, may amount to a power over every other." "The very existence," he urged, "of the local sovereignties" was "a control on the pleas for a constructive amplification of the powers of the General Government."

Two more drastic critics were friends of Jefferson and constantly stimulated by him. One of these was John Taylor of Caroline, who pronounced Marshall's doctrines to be utterly destructive of the division of powers between the two centers of government; the other was Spencer Roane, Chief Judge of the Virginia Court of Appeals, who denied that the national government derived any "constructive powers" from the supremacy clause. The designated constitutional agencies for the application of this clause, he argued, were the state judiciaries—"the judges in every state," to wit. In combatting this heresy Marshall composed one of his most powerful opinions, that in *Cohens v. Virginia.*

And many coarser voices joined in the hue and cry, and not without effect. Hardly any session of Congress convened after 1821, but witnessed some effort to curtail the powers of the Court, and the support accorded some of these in Congress reached sizeable proportions. Marshall became increasingly aware that he was fighting a losing fight.

"To men who think as you and I do," he wrote Story, toward the end of 1834, "the present is gloomy enough; and the future presents no cheering prospect. In the South . . . those who support the Executive do not support the Government. They sustain the personal power of the President, but labor incessantly to impair the legitimate powers of the Government. Those who oppose the rash and violent measures of the Executive . . . are generally the bitter enemies of Constitutional Government. Many of them are the avowed advocates of a league; and those who do not go the whole length, go a great part of the way. What can we hope for in such circumstances?"

Marshall died July 5, 1835. A few months later Justice Henry Baldwin published his *View of the Constitution,* in which he paid tribute to his late Chief Justice's qualities as expounder of the Constitution. "No commentator," he wrote, "ever followed the text more faithfully, or ever made a commentary more accordant with its strict intention and language. . . . He never brought into action the powers of his mighty mind to find some meaning in plain words . . . above the comprehension of ordinary minds. . . . He knew the framers of the Constitution, who were his compatriots"; he was himself the historian of its framing, wherefore, as its expositor, "he knew its objects, its intentions." Yet in the face of these admissions, Baldwin rejects Marshall's theory of the origin of the Constitution and the corollary doctrine of liberal construction. "The history and spirit of the times," he wrote, "admonish us that new versions of the Constitution will be promulgated to meet the varying course of political events or aspirations of power."

Baldwin's prophecy was speedily justified by the event. Within twenty-two months following Marshall's demise, the Court, having been enlarged by Congress from seven to nine Justices with the intention of watering down the still persisting Marshallian virus, received five new Justices and a new Chief Justice. Volume 11 of *Peters' Reports* reflects the juristic result of its transformation. Here occur three cases involving state laws, all of which, by Story's testimony, the late Chief Justice had stigmatized as unconstitutional. In *11 Peters* all three are sustained . . .

We move now into a new cycle of American constitutional law. The Civil War had settled the most urgent and dangerous issue of the federal relationship. A new problem had meantime arisen—that of the relation of government, and especially of the national government, to private enterprise. The problem was formulated in the first instance in the terminology of the *laissez faire* conception of governmental function. . . .

But the theory of *laissez faire* which dominated the thinking of the American Bar Association, founded in 1878, and in due course that of the Supreme Court, was a highly pretentious, highly complex construction which, in effect, presented the American people overnight, as it were, with a new doctrine of Natural Law—one which thrust the maintenance of economic competition into the status of a preferred constitutional value. Of the distinguishable elements of the theory, the oldest was a benefaction from Adam Smith's *Wealth of Nations,* which assumed a natural "economic order" whose intrinsic principles or "laws" automatically assure realization of the social welfare, provided their operation is not interfered with by judgments which are not based on the self-interest of the author thereof. This famous work appeared the same year as the Declaration of Independence, a coincidence which a president of the Association opined could only have had its origin in the mind of Deity itself. In 1857, John Stuart Mill's *Political Economy* presented the world with a revised version of the *Wealth of Nations,* and was followed two years later by Darwin's world-shattering *Origin of Species.* As elaborated particularly by Herbert Spencer and his American disciple, John Fiske, the evolutionary conception immensely reinforced the notion of governmental passivity. It was certainly reassuring to know that competition in the economic world was matched by "the struggle for existence" in the biological world, and that those who survived the latter struggle were invariably "the fittest," since that went to show that those who were most successful in economic competition were likewise "the fittest." Nor may mention be omitted of Sir Henry Maine's *Ancient Law,* which appeared two years after the *Origin of Species,* for here the evolutionary process received, so to speak, a sort of jural sanctification. "The movement of progressive societies," wrote Maine, "has hitherto been a movement from Status to Contract." If hitherto, then why not henceforth? Freedom of contract, too, was a part of the divine plan.

To return to the American Bar Association—its original membership comprised avowedly the *élite* of the American bar. Organized in the wake of the decision in *Munn v. Illinois,* which one of the members opined was a sign that the country was "gravitating toward barbarism," the Association soon became a sort of juristic sewing circle for mutual education in the gospel of *laissez faire.* Addresses and papers presented at the annual meetings iterated and reiterated the tenets of the new creed: government was essentially of private origin; the police power of the state was intended merely to implement the common law of nuisance; the right to fix prices was no part of any system of free government; "in the progress of society there is a natural tendency to freedom"; the trend of democracy is always away from regulation in the economic field; "the more advanced a nation becomes, the more will the liberty of the individual be developed."

What, however, did this signify practically? This question was answered by the president of the Association in 1892, in these words: "Can I be mistaken in claiming that Constitutional Law is the most important branch of American jurisprudence; and that the American Bar is and should be in a large degree that priestly tribe to whose hands are confided the support and defense of the Ark of the Covenant of our fathers?" . . .

And the final grist of all this grinding for the constitutional law of the period was, first, the doctrine of freedom of contract and, secondly, the doctrine that the regulation of production is exclusively reserved to the states both by the tenth amendment and by the principle of federal equilibrium. The doctrine of freedom of contract owes most to Tiedeman, who advanced the proposition that when a court was confronted with a statute restrictive of freedom of contract in the economic field, the principle that statutes are to be presumed constitutional was automatically repealed and the burden of proof was shifted to anyone who pleaded the statute.

The concept of freedom of contract is, of course, post-Marshall, being an offshoot of the substantive doctrine of due process of law, which first received important recognition in the jurisprudence of the Court in Chief Justice Taney's opinion in the *Dred Scott* case. It reached its culmination in the October term of 1935 when the Court declared in effect that a minimum wage law was beyond the competence of either the states or the national government. For our purpose we need give this concept no further attention. The other doctrine, however, that of an exclusive state power in the field of production, is immediately pertinent to the purpose of this paper.

The first important case in which this doctrine played a decisive role was the famed *Sugar Trust* case of 1895, in which the Sherman Anti-Trust Act was put to sleep for twenty years so far as its main purpose, the repression of industrial combinations, was concerned.

Early in his opinion, Chief Justice Fuller stated the fundamental rationale of the decision as follows:

> It is vital that the independence of the commercial power and of the police power, and the delimitation between them, however sometimes perplexing, should always be recognized and observed, for while the one furnishes the strongest bond of union, the other is essential to the preservation of the autonomy of the States as required by our dual form of government; and acknowledged evils, however grave and urgent they may appear to be, had better be born, than the risk be run, in the effort to suppress them, of more serious consequences by resort to expedients of even doubtful constitutionality.

In short, what was needed, the Court felt, was a hard and fast line between the two spheres of power, and in the following series of propositions it endeavored to lay down such a line: (1) production is always local, and under the exclusive domain of the states; (2) commerce among the states does not commence until goods "commence their final movement from their States of origin to that of their destination"; (3) the sale of a product is merely an incident of its production and, while capable of "bringing the operation of commerce into play," affects it only incidentally; (4) such restraint as would reach commerce, as above defined, in consequence of combinations to control production "in all its forms," would be "indirect, however inevitable and whatever its extent," and as such beyond the purview of the statute.

In the *Sugar Trust* case nullification of the legislation involved assumed, therefore, the guise—or disguise—of statutory construction. A generation later, in the first *Child Labor* case, the Court invalidated outright an act of Congress which banned from interstate commerce goods from factories in which child labor had been employed. . . .

And in *Carter v. Carter Coal Co.* decided in 1935, the Court held void on like grounds an act of Congress intended to regulate hours of labor and wages in the bituminous coal mines of the country. . . .

Thanks to the Great Depression—André Siegfried has recently pronounced it "probably the most important event in the history of the United States since the War of Independence"—this entire system of constitutional interpretation touching the federal relationship is today in ruins. It began to topple in *NLRB v. Jones & Laughlin*

Steel Corp., in which the Wagner Labor Act was sustained. This was in 1937, while the "Old Court" was still sitting. In 1941, in *United States v. Darby,* the "New Court" completed the job of demolition. The act of Congress involved was the Fair Labor Standards Act of 1938, which not only bans interstate commerce in goods produced under substandard conditions, but makes their production a penal offense against the United States if they are "intended" for interstate or foreign commerce. Here Chief Justice Stone, speaking for the unanimous Court, goes straight back to Marshall's definition of Congress' power over interstate commerce in *Gibbons v. Ogden* and to his construction of the "necessary and proper" clause in *McCulloch v. Maryland.* The former is held to sustain the power exercised in the Fair Labor Standards Act by way of prohibiting commerce; the latter is held to support the prohibition by the act of the manufacture of goods for interstate commerce except in conformity with the standards imposed by the act as to wages and hours. As to the tenth amendment, it was dismissed "as a truism that all is retained which has not been surrendered." Its addition to the Constitution altered the latter in nowise.

Summing up the effects of the *Darby* case, the late Justice Roberts said in his *Holmes Lectures* for 1951: "Of course, the effect of sustaining the Act was to place the whole matter of wages and hours of persons employed throughout the United States, with slight exceptions, under a single federal regulatory scheme and in this way completely to supersede state exercise of the police power in this field."

All in all, it is not extravagant to say that the Supreme Court has rarely, if ever, rendered a more revolutionary decision, whether it be judged for its advance over contemporary constitutional doctrine, or for its immediate legislative consequences, or for its implications for future national policy. And in the end it is Marshall's two great opinions which supply its underlying ideology. The great Chief Justice, embodied, or embalmed, in pronouncements still vital, speaks again, becomes once more the Revolutionist. Can it be supposed that if he had been present in person he would have consented willingly to be thus conscripted in the service of the New Deal? Self-exhumation of the illustrious dead is an accepted literary convention, and I claim the right to invoke it on this occasion. If the right be granted, then the answer to the above question must undoubtedly be "No." For supporting testimony I turn once more to Beveridge, for his account of the strenuous and successful fight which Marshall, with the cooperation of his critic Madison, made in the Virginia constitutional convention of 1829 against manhood suffrage and in support of the oligarchic county court system. As Beveridge phrases the matter:

> On every issue over which the factions of this convention fought, Marshall was reactionary and employed all his skill to defeat, whenever possible, the plans and purposes of the radicals. In pursuing this course he brought to bear the power of his now immense reputation for wisdom and justice. Perhaps no other phase of his life displays more strikingly his intense conservatism.

"The American Nation," Beveridge adds, "was his dream; and to the realization of it he consecrated his life." At no time, on the other hand, did he contemplate the desirability, or even the feasibility, in a free state, of greatly altering by political action the existing relations of the component elements of society. Liberty, the spacious liberty of an expanding nation, not social equality, was the lode-star of his political philosophy.

11

William W. Crosskey

William W. Crosskey, who was a professor of law at the University of Chicago, offered some unique ideas regarding the meaning of the Constitution and John Marshall's role in interpreting it. Crosskey disputed the traditional notion that Marshall dominated his colleagues and successfully imposed nationalist and loose constructionist doctrines upon the other justices. On the contrary, Crosskey insisted, Marshall consistently trimmed and compromised Federalist constitutional views in order to salvage at least some of the framers' intentions. Despite the chief justice's efforts, according to Crosskey, his service marked a period of "constitutional decay," in which the opponents of central power and vigorous government gained the dominant hand and ultimately led the nation to disunion. Crosskey's critics have dealt harshly with his conception of Federalist intentions and the extent of Marshall's failure; nevertheless, Crosskey demolished the myth of Marshall's supremacy within the Court and the myth of the consistency of his views.[1]

John Marshall was born on September 24, 1755, in what is now Fauquier County, Virginia. He died in Philadelphia, while holding the office of Chief Justice of the United States, a few weeks less than eighty years later. Thus when Americans in 1955 marked the two-hundredth anniversary of his birth, one hundred and twenty years had elapsed since he completed the judicial labors for which he is so greatly celebrated. Three other Americans preceded Marshall in the office that he held, and ten have succeeded him in that long interval since his death. Some very distinguished and able men have been Chief Justices; but, by universal consent, Marshall is recog-

[1] William W. Crosskey, "John Marshall," in Allison Dunham and Philip B. Kurland, ed., *Mr. Justice*, rev. ed. (Chicago: The University of Chicago Press, 1964), pp. 3–8, 12–20, 24, 25–26. (Footnotes deleted.) Reprinted by permission of the authors and publisher, © 1964 by The University of Chicago.

nized to stand pre-eminent—indeed, unrivaled—among them. The appelation, "the great Chief Justice," is still, as it long has been, a completely unambiguous reference to John Marshall.

I mean not to dissent from this universal view of Marshall's greatness; yet I do think that the true nature of his judicial career, particularly as it related to constitutional interpretation, has long been generally misunderstood. According to the usual view, Marshall is conceived to have dominated his associates on the Supreme Court so completely that he was able to make the constitutional decisions of that tribunal express his own ideas and nothing else. His ideas, it is further commonly assumed, were those of his political party, the Federalists. Consequently, the common view is that John Marshall was able to use, and did use, his domination of the Court to read the old Federalist constitutional views into the Court's decisions and thus to lay the foundations upon which our constitutional law ever since has rested, or—as some might wish to insist—the foundations upon which it rested until the notorious "Roosevelt Court fight" of a generation ago.

For the general prevalence of this view of John Marshall's work in constitutional law, his biographer, Albert J. Beveridge, is undoubtedly in considerable measure responsible. But such a view of Marshall's work antedated Beveridge's biography. Justice Holmes, for one, took such a view of the subject fifteen years before the first of Beveridge's volumes appeared. The occasion was the centennial, in 1901, of Marshall's inauguration as Chief Justice of the Supreme Court of the United States, and Holmes, as Chief Justice of Massachusetts, was answering a motion that the Supreme Judicial Court of that state adjourn in commemoration of the event. Holmes was not so gracious on this occasion as he usually was. He felt honest doubt about Marshall's greatness and rather inappropriately expressed it. He doubted, he said, "whether, after [Alexander] Hamilton and the Constitution itself, Marshall's work proved more than a strong intellect, a good style, personal ascendancy in his court, courage, justice and the convictions of his party." Holmes conceded, however, that it had been a "fortunate" thing that the appointment of a Chief Justice in 1801 had fallen to John Adams rather than to Thomas Jefferson, "and so g[i]ve[n] it," as he explained, "to a Federalist and loose constructionist to start the working of the Constitution. . . . These remarks of Holmes plainly evince the same view of Marshall's work that I have already mentioned as the view commonly taken: Marshall dominated the Court; he used his dominance to read Federalist party doctrines into the Constitution; and thus the basis of our constitutional law was laid. Along with these ideas, we have in the case of Holmes the further notion, which is also a common one, that the old Federalist constitutional views were based upon a "loose" construction of the Constitution.

Let me begin with this last idea. Is it true that the old Federalist constitutional views depended upon a loose construction of the Constitution? It most certainly is not. The Federalist views depended, first of all, upon a strict adherence to certain rules of documentary interpretation that were then quite generally accepted as proper. They depended, further, upon giving meaning to every single provision that the Constitution contained and, also, upon giving significance to every difference in phraseology to be found in its various provisions. The Federalist views depended, in other words, upon a literal reading of the Constitution in all its parts; and in the few cases, if there were any such, where the Federalists thought that more than one meaning was possible, the ambiguity was to be resolved, they believed, by a strict adherence to the then accepted rule of choosing the meaning that best comported with the objects, or purposes, of the Constitution as stated in the Preamble. In any ordinary use of words, the Federalist views depended, then, upon a rigorous, not a loose, construction of the document.

The views of the Federalists' opponents, the Jeffersonians, were the views that really depended upon a loose construction. The Jeffersonian views called for disregarding certain parts of the Constitution completely. These parts—the parts that then were known as "the general phrases" of the document—were to be made absolutely meaningless. Other parts were to be twisted from their original meaning in a manner unfavorable to the national powers, and limitations undeniably not contained in the document were to be read into it.

If these are the facts about the Federalist and Jeffersonian views of the Constitution, how has the notion come to be accepted, in what is known as history, that the old Federalist views depended upon a loose construction of the document? In part, this is a result of the paucity and imperfection of the records of the Federalist period. The Senate of the United States during its first five years sat behind closed doors; no record of its debates for this period exists. In addition, there was no official reporting of the debates in either house of Congress during the early years. There was, it is true, some private reporting, part of which was afterward republished in, and as, *The Annals of Congress,* in the 1830's; but these private reports from the formative period of American government are both imperfect and incomplete.

As for the courts of justice of the period—particularly the Supreme Court—the cases before them did not bring up constitutional issues that went to the essence of the old Federalist views of the subject; and this remained true, in the main, during the first six or seven years of John Marshall's Chief Justiceship, when there was still a Federalist majority on the Court. The result of all these factors, taken together, was an imperfect and meager recording of the Federalist views; they became forgotten. And because the Jeffersonians, with their usual perversity, accused the Federalists of advocating a loose construction—the offense of which they themselves were guilty—and because, furthermore, the Jeffersonians won out politically, their charge has stuck by reason of simple ignorance today as to what the old Federalist views were.

The situation I have just described has manifestly been favorable, likewise, to the rise of the misconception of John Marshall's work to which I have already alluded. But in the case of Marshall, there have been other factors at work, too. For one thing, Marshall persuaded the Court to follow the practice of delivering court opinions, instead of individual opinions, in the cases decided; and in most of the cases, Marshall wrote and delivered the Court's opinions himself, especially in those involving constitutional issues. Consequently, it is usually assumed today that everything in these opinions represents Marshall's own views and hence Federalist views. Yet, if we remember that nearly all of Marshall's constitutional opinions were delivered for a Court with a hand-picked Jeffersonian majority upon it, it is certainly undeniable that such a view of the Marshall opinions is one inherently improbable.

Such a view of the matter is, moreover, at variance with what Marshall himself described as the practice of his Court. Its practice, he indicated in 1819, was what the "course of every tribunal must necessarily be." ". . . the opinion which is to be delivered as the opinion of the court is," he said, "previously submitted to the consideration of all the judges; and if any part of the reasoning be disapproved, it must be so modified as to receive the approbation of all, before it can be delivered as the opinion of all." I do not myself see how the facts could possibly have been otherwise than as Marshall stated them; or how it can be supposed, for a moment, that he did not, in many instances, have to compromise, or give up, his own and the Federalist views of the Constitution.

There are still other factors that have contributed to the misconception of Marshall's work. One was his settled practice of not dissenting when he disagreed with the views of the Court. We have his own word for this. In *Bank of United States* v. *Dandridge*, in 1827, he said it had long been his "custom when [he] ha[d] the misfortune to differ from th[e] Court, [to] acquiesce silently in its opinion." Justice Joseph Story, who usually agreed with Marshall's constitutional views, followed the same practice. And the associate of both, Justice William Johnson, said, in 1822, "in some" instances, Marshall actually wrote and delivered the Court's opinion even "when [it was] contrary to his own Judgement and Vote." The Associate Justices were lazy, Johnson said; Marshall was willing to perform the labor of writing the opinions, and the Associates were content to let him do it.

Now, surely, in the light of this last-mentioned practice, it is perilous in the extreme to ascribe to John Marshall and hence to the old Federalists, who produced the Constitution, everything that his opinions contain. One is likewise unwarranted in making such ascriptions merely on the basis of Marshall's silent acquiescence in various of the views of his Court. Why Marshall followed the practices I have just outlined, he never explained. But the fact is that the period of his Chief Justiceship was a period of constitutional decay. Time after time, Marshall was forced into compromise or outright defeat upon what can easily be shown were his own views or else the old Federalist views of the Constitution, which, it is natural to suppose, he shared. It probably seemed to Marshall thoroughly unwise to underline such facts as these before the country and thus perhaps to encourage further attacks upon the Constitution, to the defense of which his life after 1801 was so largely devoted.

I have said that the period of John Marshall's Chief Justiceship was a period of constitutional decay. This was especially true, as respects the Supreme Court during the twenty-three year period after 1812, when most of the famous Marshall constitutional decisions were rendered; for in 1812 the Jeffersonians at last obtained a dependable majority on the Court. With the single exception of Joseph Story, all the Justices appointed up to that time during

Marshall's tenure, and nearly all of those appointed thereafter during his years on the Court, were hand-picked to vote against him on his own and the old Federalist views of the Constitution. To suppose, then, as is ordinarily done, that Marshall was able to get these men to agree with his own and the Federalist views in case after case is certainly to suppose the improbable; and it is easy to demonstrate, by a consideration of particular cases, that Marshall had no such astounding success with the Court.

It is pertinent to begin with the old Federalist doctrine that . . . over and above and beyond its specifically enumerated powers, Congress possessed a general lawmaking authority for all the objects of the government that the Preamble of the Constitution states. Authority in the government, as distinct from its different departments and officers, was deemed by the Federalists to result from this plain statement of the government's purposes, or objects. The detail in the document related, in the main, to the division of this resulting governmental power between the different departments and officers. And the Federalists pointed out that the last of Congress' enumerated powers in the Legislative Article is not only a power "to make all Laws" which shall be "necessary and proper" to carry into execution Congress' own specifically enumerated powers but a power, likewise, "to make all Laws" which shall be "necessary and proper" to carry into execution "all other Powers vested by the Constitution in the Government of the United States" or in any of its departments or officers. Mere inspection of the Constitution discloses that there are, in the document, no enumerated powers *of the government,* as distinct from the enumerated powers of its different departments and officers. The "other Powers of the Government" branch of this final power of Congress is therefore meaningless, unless it is a reference to "Powers of the Government" that are not enumerated, such as those that resulted, under eighteenth-century views, from the preambular statement of the government's general objects. This, the Federalists maintained, was what the clause had been intended to mean; and they also maintained—or, at any rate, some of them did—that the Common Defence and General Welfare Clause earlier in the same section had been intended as a separate and substantive grant of power to Congress to act for these two great purposes.

When the first Bank of the United States under the Constitution was formed in 1791, the doctrines supportive of the general national lawmaking authority of Congress were apparently the main reliance within Congress itself in support of the constitutionality of the proposed bank. Edmund Randolph, as Attorney-General, in one of the opinions he gave to President Washington, spoke of these views as "the doctrines of the friends of the bill." In these circumstances it is not surprising that the same doctrines were presented to the Supreme Court, in support of the second bank under the Constitution when in 1819 the bank's constitutionality was questioned in the case of *McCulloch* v. *Maryland*. The doctrines were presented by one of the great advocates of the time, William Pinkney, of Maryland. After hearing Pinkney's argument, Justice Joseph Story declared that "all the cobwebs of sophistry and metaphysics about State rights and State sovereignty [had been] brushed away [by Pinkney] with" what Story described as "a mighty besom." "Never [in] my whole life," said Story, have I "heard a greater speech; it was worth a journey from Salem [to Washington] to hear it."

What did Pinkney say? It is not known exactly, but it is known that he spoke for three days. Thus what we have in Wheaton's Reports is only a meager outline. The part relating to the old Federalist doctrine of general power begins by pointing out that "all the objects of the government are national objects" and by insisting that "the means [for accomplishing these objects] are, and must be, [such as are] fitted to accomplish them." "The objects," said Pinkney, "are enumerated in the constitution," whereupon he read the Preamble. "For the attainment of these vast objects," he then went on, "the government is armed with powers and faculties corresponding in magnitude." He next ran over the various congressional powers enumerated in the Legislative Article, presenting the Common Defence and General Welfare Clause as a separate substantive grant; the commerce power, apparently, as comprehensive; and the "necessary and proper" clause with emphasis upon the fact that it extended to "all the powers of the Government." Then he concluded by castigating those who "doubted [that] a government invested with such immense powers ha[d] authority to erect a corporation within the sphere of its general objects, and in order to accomplish some of those objects!" As may be perceived, the reliance in this part of Pinkney's argument was primarily upon the objects stated in the Preamble.

What did Chief Justice Marshall have to say about these old Federalist ideas in the Court's opinion? He said nothing about them; he ignored them completely, though there are one or two passages which suggest that he may originally have noticed them favorably before the opinion was seen by his judicial brethren. Instead of noticing the old Federalist ideas that Pinkney had urged, Marshall declared, early in the opinion, "this government is acknowledged by all, to be one of enumerated powers." "The principle, that it can exercise only the powers granted to it, would seem too apparent," he said, "to have required to be enforced by all those arguments which its enlightened friends, while it was depending before the people, [had] found it necessary to urge." "[T]hat principle," he flatly declared, "is now universally admitted." At least as the principle is understood today, William Pinkney did not admit it, and there were a good many other men who did not admit it at the time when Marshall wrote. Yet all the Chief Justice could do for the old ideas Pinkney had urged was to add, in the opinion, that "the question respecting the extent of the powers actually granted" was, of course, "perpetually arising, and w[ould] probably continue to arise, as long as our system sh[ould] exist." This, perhaps, could be taken as saving the question of the true interpretation of the Common Defence and General Welfare Clause and, also, of the "Powers of Government" branch of the "necessary and proper" clause, because each of these is, after all, among the enumerated, that is, the "actually granted," powers of Congress.

I have said that in 1791 the doctrine of general authority for all the purposes that the Preamble states was the main reliance, in Congress itself, in support of the constitutionality of the first Bank of the United States. This doctrine was not, however, the sole reliance of the friends of the bank bill in Congress. In addition, they relied upon the enumerated fiscal powers, especially in the light of the "necessary and proper" clause, as being themselves sufficient to warrant the proposed enactment. And there was reliance also upon Congress' power to regulate commerce as likewise sufficient in itself to warrant the intended act of incorporation. In the opinion that Alexander Hamilton gave to President Washington a little later, the commerce power and the fiscal powers were also relied upon to support the act. Unlike the men in Congress, Hamilton did not discuss the general authority of the government.

It has often been said that John Marshall's opinion in *McCulloch* v. *Maryland* is little more than a repetition of the opinion that Hamilton gave to President Washington in 1791. There are undoubtedly resemblances between these two opinions, as, indeed, there could hardly fail to be. But there are differences also; and the differences indicate, I think, that John Marshall, in 1819, was already having trouble getting some of his brethren to agree to another of the old Federalist views of the Constitution, the view that the commerce power of Congress is comprehensive.

The mere fact that there was reliance upon the commerce power by Hamilton and by the men in Congress in support of the constitutionality of the bank is, in itself, a sure indication of how these old Federalists understood this particular congressional power. For to be relevant to the subject and ground the conclusion that these men drew, the power had to be understood as complete. Had it instead been taken as subject to an interstate limitation, the conclusion they drew would not have followed; for the bank, it must be remembered, was being incorporated to carry on its business, not only in foreign and interstate commerce, but in intrastate commerce as well.

Examination of Hamilton's opinion will show that he developed his argument based on the commerce power, and relied upon it as sufficient to support his conclusion, quite as much as he did his argument based on Congress' fiscal powers. Chief Justice Marshall followed Hamilton, in *McCulloch* v. *Maryland* to the extent of citing Congress' "power to regulate commerce" as among the powers that were relevant to the case; but the Chief Justice went no further. In the actual discussion in the opinion, the reliance is wholly upon Congress' fiscal powers; and today, after more than a century's acceptance of the interstate theory of the commerce power, the very fact that Marshall cited this power as relevant in *McCulloch* v. *Maryland* is generally forgotten. The accepted doctrine is that Congress' power to incorporate national banks depends upon its fiscal powers alone.

To have grounded the conclusion in *McCulloch* v. *Maryland,* not only upon the fiscal powers of Congress, but, alternatively, upon its commerce power, would have been to make the case a far, far broader precedent in favor of congressional power than the case, as it was decided, actually was. For to have put the case upon this alternative ground would have been to recognize that Congress' power to regulate commerce was complete: that Congress could regulate all domestic as well as all foreign commerce. The situation in the *McCulloch* case was this: the Bank of the United States there involved was not the old Federalist bank incorporated in 1791; it was a newer bank created by a Jeffersonian Congress and approved by the second Jeffersonian President, James Madison, in 1816. The men of the Jeffersonian majority on Marshall's Court were apparently willing to uphold this act of their own party, but, equally apparently, they wished to do this on the narrowest possible ground. Thus the decision was put on the fiscal powers only, and the relevance of the commerce power was not developed in the case. Again, a doctrine that the old Federalists had considered relevant to Congress' incorporating a bank was excluded from the *McCulloch* case rather than read into this famous Marshall opinion.

The Chief Justice's citation of the commerce power suggests, nevertheless, that its relevancy may have been developed and relied upon in some earlier version of the opinion. Whether this actually happened or not, the citation certainly seems to indicate that Marshall himself, like Hamilton and other Federalists in 1791, considered the commerce power to be relevant; and, for reasons I have already assigned, this means that he must have regarded it as a complete power over the subject: a power to regulate all domestic as well as all foreign commerce. This surmise is borne out by what Marshall had to say two years later about this power, in *Cohens* v. *Virginia*. It was in the famous passage that begins: "[T]he United States form for many, and for most important purposes, a single nation." "In war," Marshall continued, "we are one people. In making peace, we are one people." Finally, he declared, "In all commercial regulations, we are one and the same people." "[F]or all these purposes, [America's] government," he said, "is complete; to all these objects, it is competent."

I do not see how it is possible to read these statements from the *Cohens* case as other than a plain recognition by Chief Justice Marshall that the power of Congress to regulate commerce was a complete power—that it extended to all domestic as well as all foreign commerce. The language Marshall used is totally irreconcilable with the view that he thought the power one to regulate foreign and interstate commerce only. How Marshall was able to get these statements approved by his judicial brethren in the *Cohens* case, I do not know; but the statements are there, and their meaning seems plain. Thus we may take it that John Marshall, in 1821, took the same view of the national commerce power that Alexander Hamilton and other Federalists had taken in the early 1790's.

This view, I might add, was also the view taken by the majority of the men in Congress in the 1820's. It seems, however, not to have been the view of the Jeffersonian majority on Marshall's Court. For when the famous New York steamboat monopoly case of *Gibbons* v. *Ogden* was decided in 1824, Marshall receded from the position he had taken three years earlier in *Cohens* v. *Virginia*. In the *Gibbons* case, Marshall no longer maintained that the United States formed a single nation as to 'all commercial regulations." Instead, though referring to the language of the Constitution as "comprehensive," he declared that the power it gave might "very properly be restricted to that commerce which concerns more States than one." Again, Marshall failed to read into one of the Court's decisions what it is clear was his own and an old Federalist view of the Constitution.

But although that fact is certain, it is a mistake to suppose, as is frequently done, that in the Gibbons case Marshall interpreted the commerce power in the meager dimensions in which that power existed during the major part of subsequent American history. In other words, it is a mistake to suppose that Marshall in the *Gibbons* case interpreted Congress' internal power over commerce as a power to regulate interstate commerce only. The Chief Justice said that the power was being restricted to "that commerce which concerns more States than one"; and his opinion makes abundantly clear what he meant by these words. He meant by them all commerce of a domestic kind that was of interest, or importance, to more than a single state; and he meant this whether the particular commerce was interstate or not. Marshall said, moreover, that with respect to all such commerce, Congress' power was "plenary"—"as absolut[e]," he declared, "as [a commerce power] would be in a single government." And whenever Congress acted under this great power, any conflicting state law must yield whether the law in question was one for the regulation of a state's own purely domestic commerce or one for the regulation of its system of internal police.

That *Gibbons* v. *Ogden* was not contemporaneously understood as adopting the interstate theory of the commerce power is shown, moreover, by what happened in the following year, in the state of New York. The interstate theory was not then entirely unknown. It had been devised, somewhat earlier, by lawyers for the New York steamboat monopoly and had been applied by the highest court of the state, in 1812, to uphold the monopoly as between citizens of the state, in respect to traffic between the New York cities of New York and Albany. This was in the case of *Livingston* v. *Van Ingen,* a case which, because the defendants were bought off by the successful plaintiffs, was not appealed to the Supreme Court of the United States. *Gibbons* v. *Ogden,* though not adopting the interstate theory, had actually involved steamboat movements between New York and New Jersey. The decision, then, left technically open the question whether the New York monopoly law was still good with respect to movements such as had been involved in the *Van Ingen* case, that is, with respect to movements wholly within the state. A case was accordingly begun in the New York courts, a few weeks after the *Gibbons* decision, to settle this question. Under the title of *North River Steamboat Company* v. *Livingston,* the case was carried to the highest court of the state in 1825. The New York court thereupon overruled the interstate doctrine of its earlier decision and, on the authority of the *Gibbons* case, brought the New York steamboat monopoly completely to an end, both in intrastate and interstate commerce.

It is needless to say that the New York court would never have taken such action had it understood the Supreme Court's decision of the preceding year as one adopting the interstate theory of the commerce power. But if the interstate theory did not originate in *Gibbons* v. *Ogden,* it may be asked how, and when, the theory did originate. The answer is that the theory was read into John Marshall's decision in the *Gibbons* case by his Jacksonian successor, Roger Brooke Taney. Marshall's doctrine of plenary national supremacy, which he had announced so clearly in the *Gibbons* case, was overturned within two years of his death by the Jacksonian Court. This occurred in *New York* v. *Miln,* in 1837, when it was indicated by the Court that the whole field of internal police was free of the national supremacy. Ten years later Chief Justice Taney blew this unwarranted concept up to include the regulation of all intrastate commerce. He did this in his oft-quoted definition of the states' police powers, in the License cases of 1847.

The "police power of a State," said Chief Justice Taney, is "the power of sovereignty, the power to govern men and things within the limits of [a state's] dominions." Then, in specific reference to the subject of commerce, he added that "every State [might] regulate its own internal traffic, according to its own judgment," and "free," he declared, "from any controlling power on the part of the general government." He was "not aware," he added, "that these principles ha[d] ever been questioned." One might suppose from this statement that Chief Justice Taney had never read *Gibbons* v. *Ogden;* but his own memories went back to the founding of the government, and we may feel quite sure he knew exactly what he was about. His statements, at any rate, constitute, I believe, the earliest evidence of adherence to the interstate theory of the commerce power to be found in the Supreme Court's reports. The theory was not actually applied against Congress until 1869. . . .

It would be possible to add to the foregoing instances; but enough has been said, I hope, to convince the reader that the usual view of John Marshall's career is hardly tenable. John Marshall did not carry on a continual frontal assault, uniformly successful, upon the subversive principles of Jeffersonianism. Instead, he fought a long and stubborn rearguard action to defend the Constitution against those principles. And it was, on the whole, a losing fight. Time after time during his long career, Marshall was forced into compromise or defeat; and the result was a pretty complete transformation of the Constitution by the date of his death.

No one, it may be added, was more aware of what was going on than John Marshall. As his biographer has shown from the letters of his closing years, Marshall died almost in despair of the future of the Union. He was convinced that the South—his own state of Virginia in particular—had determined to convert the Union into a loose confederation. And that he was not far wrong is shown by the action I have already noted of the southerners who dominated the Taney Court that came into power upon Marshall's death in 1835. The Taney Court's initial action, in substituting the principle of the inviolability of the states' police powers for Marshall's principle of plenary national supremacy, was greeted by one of the nationalists of the time as "a return to the principles of the Articles of Confederation." Such, there can be no doubt, it truly was, especially after the concept of state police power was blown up to include the regulation of all intrastate commerce, as it was in the *License Cases* of 1847.

These two principles—the interstate theory of Congress' power over commerce and the inviolability of the police powers of the states—were certainly basic to American constitutional law until very recent times; and these principles derived, not from the decisions of John Marshall, but from unjustified glosses upon his decisions by Roger Brooke Taney and the Jacksonian Court that came into power upon Marshall's death. So far, moreover, as constitutional law actually has been based on Marshall's decisions, it has involved much more of Jeffersonianism than of federalism, much more of the views of Marshall's associates on the Court than of Marshall's own ideas. And the fragments of federalism that did survive in the Marshall decisions represented, in the main, no more than what Marshall's associates felt compelled to agree to, in order to reach results that they desired to reach on other grounds. In saying these things, I do not mean to imply that John Marshall had no victories at all, for this would not be true; but I do mean to say that on the great fundamental theses of federalism—the theses that went to the very character of the government, the theses that I have here reviewed—John Marshall was defeated, either by his own Court or by the Taney Court that succeeded him.

Does this conclusion impugn Marshall's claim to greatness? I can only say that, so far as I am concerned, I do not think it does. A man may be great in tragedy as well as triumph, in defeat as well as victory. And since there was, it seems to me, much more of tragedy and defeat than of triumph and victory in John Marshall's career as defender of the Constitution, the traditional estimate of the nature of his career ought, I think, to be revised to show him as he truly was. His greatness, clearly, was not that of triumphant victory. It was a greatness that consisted in devoting half a lifetime to a cause in which he profoundly believed; in faithful service to that cause in the face of overwhelming odds; in unflagging courage in the face of those odds and in the face of constantly recurring defeats. There can be no doubt, moreover, that John Marshall, in spite of the circumstances in which he worked, accomplished a very great deal in the way of minimizing damage; that it was, indeed, a "fortunate" thing, as Oliver Wendell Holmes observed, in 1901, that it fell to Marshall, and not to an appointee of Thomas Jefferson, to serve in the critical early years of the nineteenth century as Chief Justice of the United States. The circumstance, I think, probably saved the Union.

Although I take a very different view of Marshall's work than is usually taken, he still remains to me "the great Chief Justice." There is not one of his predecessors, not one of those who succeeded him, that I should think, for a moment, of nominating in his place.

12
Robert K. Faulkner

*Unlike Crosskey, Robert Faulkner is a warm, en-
thusiastic admirer of Marshall's work and achievement. Moreover, Faulkner finds that Marshall faithfully reflected the
intentions of the framers. This selection is drawn from Faulkner's full-length study of the sources and application of Marshall's constitutional thought. In a rigorous analysis of Marshall's words and thoughts, Faulkner offers some healthy cor-
rectives for our awareness of Marshall, particularly in that he
does not misconstrue or underestimate the extent of the chief
justice's commitment to fundamental constitutional maxims.
The following essay summarizes Marshall's constitutional understanding and his implementation of judicial review to preserve that understanding.[1]*

It is fitting to conclude a study of Marshall's jurisprudence by
considering how the famous power of judicial review completes
his liberal republicanism. Marshall's life culminated, as is well
known, in a vivifying of the Supreme Court. He is rightly regarded,
as we too have treated him, not as philosopher or framer, nor even
as statesman in the usual sense, but as "the great Chief Justice"
and as "Expounder of the Constitution." It is natural that his jurisprudence, attuned to the regime of 1788, should be rounded out in
his treatment of the Constitution as fundamental law and, especially, of the Supreme Court as its authoritative interpreter. Well
might the Court be dignified with the old metaphor of keystone of
the Republic. It was not the most massive stone, nor the most con-
spicuous, but it was, Marshall thought, the crowning one that held
the others in place. . . .
According to Marshall the Constitution of 1788 was to be an

[1] From the "Court and Constitution in the Republic," in Robert K. Faulkner,
The Jurisprudence of John Marshall (copyright © 1968 by Princeton University
Press), pp. 193–212. (Footnotes deleted.) Reprinted by permission of Princeton
University Press.

effectual guide to government, not merely a blueprint. It was
fundamental law no less than fundamental plan. The permanence
and authority of the charter played an integral part, in fact, in the
whole scheme of government. It guaranteed the continued working
of that ingenious system of public powers and private energies introduced by the "enlightened" philosophers. In accord with one of
Locke's more technical distinctions, the Americans' charter of 1788
might be said to correspond to the second contract whereby a people
proceeds to erect governing arrangements through the "original constitution" of a legislature. This "legislature is not only the supreme
power of the commonwealth," Locke wrote, "but sacred and un-
alterable in the hands where the community have once placed it."
"The power of the legislature," Locke dwelled on his lesson once
again, "being derived from the people by a positive voluntary grant
and institution, can be no other than what that positive grant conveyed. . . ."

By the very nature of the institutions thus established, the government erected is a limited government. . . . And in several opinions on domestic and international law, notably that of *Fletcher* v.
Peck. . . . Marshall indicated that "general principles of law"
might restrain political authority even in the absence of express
provisions.

The distinguishing excellence of the Americans' basic law, however, was explicit definition and limitation of governmental powers.
It was this written document that had been "deemed" by Americans, as Marshall interpreted their thoughts, "the greatest improvement on political institutions." Again the Americans were following
in their political improvements the spirit of Locke, and perhaps
even the letter. At the establishment of a new government, the liberal philosopher had advised, the people should insist on "express
conditions limiting or regulating" governmental powers. The Americans did so, according to Marshall's terse account in *Marbury* v.
Madison.

> This original and supreme will [of the people] organizes the govern-
> ment, and assigns, to different departments, their respective powers.
> It may either stop here; or establish certain limits not to be tran-
> scended by those departments.
> The government of the United States is of the latter description.

The powers of the legislature are defined, and limited; and that those limits may not be mistaken, or forgotten, the constitution is written.

Once established the Constitution was not to be varied in its fundamentals. This no doubt sounds strange to those educated in sociological jurisprudence, who believe society is always changing, or rather progressing, and that the law too must constantly vary to keep up with society. Marshall was not unaware of the development of industry and population which the country was about to undergo. Yet he thought this in good part the product of the Constitution's unchanging fundamentals. Development followed from sound laws; it was not a "historical process" to which man is inevitably fated. Hence the importance in Marshall's eyes, apart from the intrinsic worth of man's rights, of making permanent the framers' sound laws.

It is quite true that Marshall affirmed "we must never forget that it is a constitution we are expounding." But this Marshallian maxim so well known to modern jurists has been grossly, if perhaps necessarily, twisted by commentators from the meaning Marshall gave it. It means, as he said in *McCulloch* v. *Maryland,* that the government's powers are to be interpreted in accord with the tasks posed by its objects. Marshall's emphasis upon the great "exigencies" which the government must confront in providing, say, for the national defense, need not be rehearsed. Subordinate objects, like a national bank, and powers, like that to charter a national bank, may be deduced from the "great objects" of the chief powers. But this in no way implies that the objects themselves, or the basic kinds of powers, may change or "evolve." Flexibility there is, but flexibility as to only the means in accord with the spirit of a Lockean Constitution. "Its means are adequate to its ends," wrote Marshall, and he intended to say no more. The famous passage that we have already quoted must be taken in all its parts: "Let the end be legitimate, let it be within the scope of the constitution, and all means which are appropriate, which are plainly adapted to that end, which are not prohibited, but consist with the letter and spirit of the constitution, are constitutional." Marshall's understanding of the Constitution's powers must be interpreted . . . according to the view of the country's objects . . . ". . . Should Congress," he wrote

a bit later in the McCulloch opinion, "in the execution of its
powers, adopt measures which are prohibited by the constitution;
or should Congress, under the pretext of executing its powers pass
laws for the accomplishment of objects not intrusted to the government, it would become the painful duty of this tribunal, should a
case requiring such a decision come before it, to say that such an
act was not the law of the land." We need repeat that there is no
contradiction between Marshall's opinion in the McCulloch case,
elaborating Congress's political powers, and that in *Marbury* v.
Madison, defining the obligation of the President to obey strictly a
congressional act upon which individual rights depend. There is
only the difference of tenor which accords with liberalism's generous
supply of power for the political departments' indirect sustenance
of individual rights, and with its jealous protection of the rights
themselves. In both cases, it is presumed that the Constitution's
public law and private law is to endure.

Marshall's supposition that law so serviceable to the people's interests must be supposed permanent is perfectly visible in his treatment of the amending power. Apart from the last resort of revolution, that provision is the sole legitimate way that the ultimately
sovereign people could vary the fundamentals of the government to
which they had delegated so many of their sovereign powers. "A
state without the means of some change is without the means of its
preservation" is a good Burkean maxim. Marshall's interpretation
of the amending power amounts to scarcely more. The provision is
but another mode, he wrote, of assuring "immortality to [the framers'] work." It allows the variations in detail which changing circumstances might require. So long as their government is not oppressive,
the people are supposed to have essentially exhausted their own
exercise of sovereignty with the authoritative, and even presump-
tively immortal, expression of their will embodied in the Constitution.

> That the people have an original right to establish, for their future
> government, such principles as, in their opinion, shall most conduce
> to their own happiness, is the basis, on which the whole American
> fabric has been erected. The exercise of this original right is a very
> great exertion; nor can it, nor ought it to be frequently repeated.
> The principles, therefore, so established, are deemed fundamental.
> And as the authority, from which they proceed is supreme, and, can
> seldom act, they are designed to be permanent.

If a written constitution was "the greatest improvement on political institutions," in America this improvement would inevitably be republican in character. Any rule of law tends to moderate government and thus the preponderant political force of the community governed. That force belonged in the United States to the democratic majority. Thus the American constitution tended to moderate the American democracy with the elaborate liberal mechanism of rights and powers characteristic, together with popular institutions, of Marshall's republicanism. "With the exceptions . . . of Connecticut and Rhode Island, whose systems had ever been in high degree democratic," commented the historian Marshall on the spread of the "improvement" through the first state constitutions, "the hitherto untried principle was adopted, of limiting the departments of government by a written constitution, prescribing bounds not to be transcended by the legislature itself."

Indeed, the Constitution's somewhat undemocratic character was apparent in its very origin. The document had been framed not by the many, but by the "enlightened," "illustrious," "statesmen and patriots" of the Federal Convention. Marshall always interpreted the instrument according to their intentions, not in light of the opinions expressed in the Ratifying Conventions. The people generally had only consented to what the few had proposed. Strictly speaking, the many, the people in a democratic sense, did not even consent to it. The Constitution was ratified by "the best talents of the several states," natural if indeed elected representatives of the "people" understood in Marshall's republican sense. "Had the influence of character been removed," it will be remembered, "the intrinsic merits of the instrument would not have secured its adoption" in the face of popular distrust.

JUDICIAL REVIEW

To be more than weak pretensions the Constitution's claims to permanence obviously had to be enforced. Just as obviously, Marshall thought, the task was principally the Supreme Court's. With the nation's highest judicial authority rested the chief responsibility for preserving a republican fundamental law in a country strongly tending towards democracy. No doubt "the maintenance of the principles established in the constitution" was the duty of all the departments. Still, the judiciary's role was first in dignity and authority, for it was to determine the principles to be guarded. While the Americans were to be ruled by a fundamental law, the courts alone, according to Marshall, authoritatively expounded the law's meaning and application. In effect the judiciary ruled the political departments by defining the outlines of their duties.

Although the Court's predominance over the political branches is a necessary implication of Marshall's famous argument in *Marbury* v. *Madison,* it is by no means the obvious theme. Marshall never asserted that the Court could rule the other departments in their political tasks. He even rejected indignantly the imputation to the Court of any such view. "Questions in their nature political, or which are, by the constitution and laws, submitted to the political departments, can never be made in this court." There is, however, a catch in this statement that we have noted. It is, according to the Marbury opinion, the judiciary that decides finally which questions are "in their nature political," or which are indeed, "by the constitution and laws," submitted to the political departments. While the courts might not meddle in the political sphere, they alone determine how far the forbidden sphere extends. By their authority to interpret the Constitution and laws they can limit law-maker and law-executor alike. The national courts thus not only judge under the laws but magisterially preside over them.

The Marshallian reasoning which supports this authority, then unique among great nations, is not only as magisterial but as obscure as his statement of the authority itself. With a diffidence which has emboldened his friends and exasperated his enemies, the Chief Justice declared the questions involved "not of an intricacy proportioned" to the interest which had somehow been aroused. "It seems only necessary to recognize certain principles, supposed to have been long and well established, to decide it." And then Marshall read his countrymen a terse primer on the "theory . . . essentially attached to a written constitution."

Before we show the dependence of this theory on Marshall's republicanism, it is necessary to caution the reader against another kind of political explanation so common in this age of reductionism: the tendency to reduce Marshall's thoughts to his politics in a narrowly partisan sense. The doctrines of *Marbury* v. *Madison* are sometimes treated as the Chief Justice's last minute expedient to foil the on-rushing Jeffersonians. That he wanted to foil the Jeffersonians is undoubtedly true. That he manipulated the case of

Marbury v. *Madison* to arrange an ingenious opportunity to affirm judicial review is probably true, although the persuasive inferences of Corwin and others have yet to be accompanied by other evidence. Whatever doubts may surround the occasion for his remarks, however, the convictions expressed are those which he had long held. In 1798 he had presumed that it was the "province" and "duty" of "the judges of the United States" to construe the fundamental law. In his first public deliberations on the Constitution at the Virginia Ratifying Convention, long before Jefferson and his Republicans were a source of anxiety, Marshall had said, "If [the government of the United States] were to make a law not warranted by any of the powers enumerated, it would be considered by the judges as an infringement of the Constitution which they are to guard. They would not consider such a law as coming under their jurisdiction. They would declare it void."

Considering the settled nature of Marshall's convictions on the judiciary's authority, it is proper to understand his defense of judicial review not as mere partisan maneuver but in the perspective of his whole jurisprudence. This explanation conforms to the confident manner in which Marshall himself argued along lines "supposed to have been long and well established." It is confirmed as well by the conclusions of Corwin in the most assiduous investigation of judicial review. "The power rests upon certain general principles thought by its framers to have been embodied in the Constitution." These principles underlie Marshall's argument in particular, as well as the framers' views in general. It is true, however, that the skimpy and sanguine shape of the argument in *Marbury* v. *Madison* cannot be fully explained by Marshall's deeper premises. To understand the argument's peculiarities of form, one is compelled to return once again to the political circumstances of the time.

The discussion which follows does more than elaborate the basic and explicit doctrines of the Chief Justice's argument. Corwin has already done that. I wish to show that those doctrines presuppose a republican role for the Court. In unearthing these political premises I have found nothing more helpful than the biting criticisms of Justice John B. Gibson of Pennsylvania. The conclusion of constitutional scholars that Gibson's opinion in *Eakin* v. *Raub* [1825] contains the most compelling analysis of *Marbury* v. *Madison,* is not matched, so far as I know, by any thorough confrontation of Marshall's reasoning with Gibson's rebuttal, finally measuring the one by the other. The Pennsylvania judge offered the careful and systematic dissection that the more influential Jefferson never made.

To begin with, Gibson's opinion helps to tear away the puzzling persuasiveness resulting from the very order of Marshall's argument. The Chief Justice turned to consider the Court's authority to void legislation as unconstitutional only after he had adjudged unconstitutional a certain section of the Judiciary Act of 1789. He then divided the rest of his opinion into a discussion of two questions. First, "whether an act, repugnant to the constitution, can become the law of the land," and, second, whether an unconstitutional act does, "notwithstanding its invalidity, bind the courts, and oblige them to give it effect." Gibson showed that this procedure begs the question. At every step Marshall assumed the propriety of an independent judicial appraisal of an act's constitutionality, whereas the Court's authority to engage in such a judgment is precisely the issue in dispute. In his formulation of the first question, for example, the Chief Justice assumed that the Court can take cognizance of conflict between law and Constitution. As Gibson remarks, "to affirm that the Judiciary has a right to judge of the existence of such a collision, is to take for granted the very thing to be proved. And that a very cogent argument may be made in this way, I am not disposed to deny; for no conclusions are so strong as those that are drawn from the *petitio principii.*"

To insist that Marshall's arrangement of his discussion begs the question, however, is not to show that his opinion is devoid of relevant discussion. This Gibson realized full well. Whatever the mere prejudices which existed on the subject generally—and by 1825 Gibson considered the doctrine of judicial review "a professional dogma" which "universally has been assumed by the *American courts*"—the Chief Justice at least could be depended upon to offer an argument. "Although the right in question has all along been claimed by the judiciary, no judge has ventured to discuss it, except Chief Justice Marshall. . . ." The Marshallian syllogism supporting judicial review has been long familiar. The laws of a country are to be construed by its courts; the Constitution is a law of the United States; therefore, the Constitution is to be interpreted by the courts of the United States and finally by its highest court.

> It is emphatically [Marshall wrote in *Marbury* v. *Madison*] the province and duty of the judicial department to say what the law is. Those who apply the rule to particular cases, must of necessity

expound and interpret that rule. If two laws conflict with each other, the courts must decide on the operation of each.

So if a law be in opposition to the constitution; if both the law and the constitution apply to a particular case, so that the court must either decide that case conformably to the law, disregarding the constitution; or conformably to the constitution, disregarding the law; the court must determine which of these conflicting rules governs the case. This is of the very essence of judicial duty.

If then the courts are to regard the constitution; and the constitution is superior to any ordinary act of the legislature; the constitution, and not such ordinary act, must govern the case to which they both apply.

Now there is a certain difficulty in this beguiling syllogism which Gibson brings out very clearly indeed, a difficulty according to Marshall's own liberalism. The Pennsylvania judge agreed with Marshall's major and minor premises—but only with a significant qualification. Granted that it is "emphatically the business of the judiciary to ascertain and pronounce what the law is"; this business, however, is limited as a rule to "civil," and does not include "political," law. Indeed, the Constitution is a law of the United States, but it is not "an act of ordinary legislation, by the appropriate organ of the government." It is instead "an act of extraordinary legislation, by which the people establish the structure and mechanism of their government, and in which they prescribe fundamental rules to regulate the motion of the several parts." The Constitution is "political law" *par excellence*. Thus, Gibson concluded, the judiciary is by no means an appropriate interpreter of the Constitution.

The force of Gibson's argument is not difficult to see, and it has been popularized by such students of the Court as Charles Grove Haines. The Pennsylvania judge was like Marshall in being a Lockean liberal, if . . . of a somewhat more democratic type, and he strikes with the Chief Justice's own liberal weapons. Neither Locke nor Hume nor even Montesquieu had ever recommended a power in the courts comparable to judicial review. . . . Marshall himself limit[ed] the judiciary's authority to "legal" rather than "political" matters. He granted on many occasions, moreover, that certain matters in form legal, such as treaties among nations, were in fact political. The success of Marshall's once-famous speech in Congress on the Jonathan Robbins affair turned upon a distinction between legal questions reserved to the judiciary, and questions involving points of law which were nevertheless "questions of political

law, proper to be decided by the executive, and not by the courts."
Although Marshall never called the Constitution itself a political
law, he certainly distinguished it very forcefully indeed, in *McCulloch* v. *Maryland*, from "an ordinary legal code." The whole point
of the now familiar remark, "We must never forget that it is a constitution we are expounding," depends upon the peculiar character
of the fundamental law. The Court's opinion, he wrote in *McCulloch* v. *Maryland*, might "essentially influence the great operations
of government." After all, in *Marbury* v. *Madison* itself, Marshall
had deemed a fixed Constitution the greatest improvement in
"political institutions." To repeat, Gibson's critique strikes home
in Marshall's own liberal premises.

If Gibson's argument has great force, however, it is by no means
decisive. For he himself admits exceptions, both express and implied, to the judiciary's obligation to obey the political departments'
constructions of the Constitution. The judiciary might engage in
review of legislation, albeit only by "producing a direct authority
for it in the constitution, either in terms or by irresistible implication from the nature of the government. . . ."

Through such holes it might seem that Marshall could drive his
whole argument. Indeed, the Chief Justice relied chiefly on implications of the government's nature, rather than express provisions.
Only at the conclusion of his discussion did he refer to several
explicit limitations upon the national government, and these are
but "illustrations" by means of which his "theory" of government
is "confirmed" and "strengthened."

The gist of the theory Marshall finds "essentially attached to a
written constitution" is the necessity for effectual limitation of the
legislature. At every crucial point in Marshall's reasoning, when he
is establishing that a law contrary to the Constitution is void, or
when he insists that a void law must be ignored by the judges, the
spectre of an unchecked legislative department is brought forth to
justify Marshall's alternative. The judges, to quote the most illu-
minating passage, must follow the Constitution in preference to
conflicting law, or else they "would be giving to the legislature a
practical and real omnipotence, with the same breath which professes to restrict their powers within narrow limits." That "or else"
provides the key to Marshall's argument and to his rhetorical skill,
in *Marbury* v. *Madison*. It is the Court's role as "balancer" that is
used to justify judicial review. Marshall's argument proceeds by

pointing to the horrors of "legislative omnipotence," elevating judicial potency only (as it might appear) inadvertently and hence inconspicuously.

It is, however, just such an elevation of the Court's power that Gibson believed unjustifiable. While he admitted exceptions to his maxim that courts can't overrule the other departments, he showed himself disposed to limit the exceptions to those authorized by explicit provisions, and to confine such provisions to those expressly applicable to the Judiciary Department. Gibson would emphatically restrict the courts to "civil" affairs, and allow them to overrule other departments only where the Constitution assigns civil duties directly to the judiciary. There is a manifest difference from Marshall, who had taken the Constitution's limits on every department as indicative of the Court's authority to enforce the whole Constitution. Either the Courts enforce, "or else. . . ."

The difference as to the Court's sphere is occasioned by Gibson's very different theory of the government's nature, a theory exalting the legislature rather than fearing it. Again Gibson's doctrine reminds us of Marshall's own liberalism. . . . All the organs of government "are of equal capacity; or, if not, each must be supposed to have superior capacity only for those things which peculiarly belong to it. . . ." And hence the limits on each department are to be interpreted by that department. "Legislation," to take the key case, "peculiarly involves the consideration of those limitations which are put on the law-making power. . . ." The legislature's peculiar capacity, moreover, makes it superior to that of any other department. In the law-making branch is vested the power to *command,* whereas the other departments are but "governed by prescribed rules and exercise no power of volition." "The very definition of law, which is said to be 'a rule of civil conduct prescribed by the supreme power in the state,' shows the intrinsic superiority of the legislature." For Gibson as for Locke, the legislature was not merely one department but the "sovereign" department.

Yet a reply to Gibson is possible on liberal grounds, if not in a conventionally liberal manner. Sovereign legislative power is granted, it will be recalled, not as an end in itself, but as a means to the security of life, liberty, and property. Suppose that in America's robustly popular circumstances the liberal means do not fit the liberal end, that an unchecked legislature does not protect the rights of persons and property but endangers them. Might not a judicial supervision of the legislature be introduced? One of Corwin's early articles demonstrates that it was precisely the post-Revolutionary democratic excesses of popular state legislatures that led to a gradual public acceptance of judicial correction of their acts, although not quite to the unambiguous devotion to judicial review exhibited by the classic *Federalist* 78 and by Marshall. Judicial review, not recommended by the philosophers of liberalism, nevertheless emerged in popular America as a revision required by liberal ends.

It is quite clear that such judicial supervision would involve a certain amount of judgment as to matters of "policy," as to the legitimacy of the political departments' exercise of their powers. Courts perhaps lack the "superior capacity" of the legislature for such judgments. Yet this difficulty does not dispose of the matter. For the broad outlines of political policy were defined, as Marshall thought, by natural public law, an integral part of that liberal jurisprudence with which Courts educated by Blackstone were familiar. Particular details were to be left in any event to the discretion of executive and legislature. Thus the original premises of Marshall's argument can be more deeply appreciated. Although the Constitution was a political law, its politics were to be guided by natural public law. The judges' training in liberal jurisprudence made them at least as fit as the legislature, the more democratic legislature, to discern the natural constitution behind the written Constitution. Thus the Courts were competent to play the ambiguously political checking role which the "theory" of American government demanded from them.

It is with respect to those demands that Gibson finally differed. The Pennsylvania judge even agreed that some counter-balancing power was needed to render the Constitution's written limitations more than vain admonitions. That check should be provided by the people, however, not by the judges. "The notion of a complication of counter checks has been carried to an extent in theory," Gibson remarked, "of which the framers of the constitution never dreamt." An error by the judges in interpreting the Constitution could be corrected only by "the extraordinary medium of a convention," whereas "an error by the legislature admits of a remedy . . . in the ordinary exercise of the right of suffrage." "It rests with the people, in whom full and absolute sovereign power resides, to correct abuses in legislation." It is finally Gibson's democracy, the active role which he found assigned to the people in the constitutional system, that caused his objection to judicial review. "It is a postulate in the theory of our government, and the very basis of its superstructure," he wrote when his argument had reached its crucial turn, "that the people are wise, virtuous, and competent to manage their own affairs." Yet this "postulate" was not shared by the dominant framers. Their experience under the Articles had left them with less than Gibson's confidence in the people. Indeed they had feared especially the more democratic legislatures. Assuming a basically popular country, the framers set forth a liberal separation of powers arranged so as to trim out the people's excesses. They sought balanced government, balanced against the more democratic legislature especially. For Marshall, as for the framers, the judiciary was an integral part of a government designed in good part to minimize the people's vices, not merely to depend upon their virtues. It was because of Marshall's republicanism, then, that he was able to blithely ignore the "implications for democracy" which bother many now and bothered Gibson then.

I have tried to show the essential presuppositions underlying Marshall's argument in *Marbury* v. *Madison*. Yet the brief and even skimpy form which the argument takes has yet to be explained. In good part, the deeper and more republican assumptions never appear. Marshall was instead content to set forth in memorable sentences only the most obvious principles justifying judicial review. Why did he not probe deeper? Surely the reason lies not in his ignorance. He knew *The Federalist*. In 78 Hamilton had made explicit enough the connection between independent judges, judicial review, and the suppression of those "ill humours which the arts of designing men, or the influence of particular conjunctures, sometimes disseminate among the people themselves, and which . . . have a tendency . . . to occasion dangerous innovations in the government, and serious oppressions of the minor party in the community." The superiority of what Corwin justly calls *The Federalist*'s "classic" discussion is precisely owing to its development of the connection between judicial review and the Constitution's liberal republicanism. Why did not Marshall himself develop this connection, which makes intelligible the weight he puts upon "certain principles, supposed to have been long and well established"? His abilities were not wanting, nor was the judiciary's place as he wished it perfectly appreciated in the Jeffersonian climate of 1803.

Perhaps the reason lies in Marshall's caution in the face of the democratic inclinations of his audience. One does not preach democracy's limitations to democrats and expect thus to leaven democracy. The more likely effect in Marshall's own situation would have been the Court's overthrow. The effect of *Marbury* v. *Madison* was in fact far different. Charles Warren showed that, while Marshall's discussion consoled and encouraged the Federalist press, it failed to arouse a reciprocal reaction even in "the most bitterly partisan Republican papers." Jefferson himself was repeatedly to bemoan the acceptance of Marshall's argument among bench and bar. Part of the reason for its appeal surely lay in the moderate American public's devotion to many of the moderating principles on which Marshall relied. Yet that is insufficient. The public had displayed other tendencies, which dragged law and legal principles in other than Marshallian directions. An adequate explanation must then take into account the rhetorical skill of Marshall's own opinion. The Chief Justice's ingenuity lay in building his doctrines into the susceptible side of the Americans' dispositions, thus reducing the other in spite of itself. Marshall did not, like Justice Samuel Chase, cast the republican judiciary into the teeth of the democrats. Not one express criticism of democracy can be found in the Chief Justice's judicial opinions. Instead he insinuated his judiciary into their minds. The task did not call for an exhaustively enlightening discussion. It demanded a prudently cautious inculcation in memorable phrases of only those principles necessary for public belief in order that judicial review be sustained. Unlike Hamilton, Marshall wrote not for the "best talents of the several states" who were considering the Constitution, but for the considerably more democratically inclined public of Jeffersonian America.

The discussion comes full circle, then. Beginning with a search for the Marshallian reasoning which is intellectually necessary but not apparent, we understand from the argument's character why it had to be left implicit. For a politics better than the common wish, or even instrumental to the common desires, neither true speech nor wisdom, to say nothing of free speech, is sufficient. Statesmanship employing rhetoric is still required. It must be of a kind that constructs the political edifice on the foundations provided by common opinion, and thus is able to shape the public mind. Such was Marshall's achievement in establishing judicial review.

Afterword

Relative calm and quiet surrounded Marshall's last years as chief justice. In 1831, at the age of seventy-six, he went to Philadelphia and submitted himself to a laborious, dangerous operation for the removal of bladder stones. During his visit, the Philadelphia bar honored him with a number of resolutions praising his work. Unable to respond with a personal appearance, Marshall gratefully acknowledged the bar's recognition with what he must have considered his valedictory. He proudly claimed that he and his associates had "never sought to enlarge the judicial power beyond its proper bounds, nor feared to carry it to the fullest extent that duty required."

Marshall had done his duty and, perhaps, he could look back with the satisfaction that he had given his best. But the closing years of his life could not have been altogether happy for him. The harmonious social and professional relationships, carefully nourished during nearly three decades on the Court, had dissolved, as illness, death, and new appointees changed the composition of the bench. Prolonged absences by some of the justices, and deep divisions among them, often prevented the resolution of important cases. The first great constitutional cases settled, in 1837, under Marshall's successor, Roger B. Taney, had been argued as far back as 1831, four years before Marshall's death. In two of them, *New York* v. *Miln* and *Briscoe* v. *Bank of Kentucky* (involving, respectively, state power over foreign commerce and state-backed paper currency), it seems certain that Marshall had failed to swing a majority behind his views. By 1837, key personnel changes resulted in decisions apparently contrary to the views Marshall had advocated.

The instability within the Supreme Court mirrored the unrest and uncertain course of the nation. In the states, pressures increased for more popular participation in politics and the electoral process. Over great opposition from an older generation, virtually every state revised its constitution in this period. In 1829, Marshall, along with his friends, James Madison and James Monroe, served as a delegate to the Virginia convention. He played a leading part in preventing a broad expansion of the suffrage, and, generally, he supported retention of the archaic institutions that made Virginia's government one of the least representative in the nation. However dismayed Marshall may have been with the drive for more democracy, he must have viewed the growing sectionalism and concurrent threats of disunion with even greater chagrin.

The partisan attacks on Marshall and his colleagues largely had subsided by this time. The chief justice himself already was an object of veneration, a living representative of the revolutionary patriots and the founding fathers of the Constitution. Yet he also was something of an anachronism, as his sentiments for the Union and firm belief in national supremacy appeared decidedly out of fashion. In *Cohens* v. *Virginia,* in 1821, Marshall emphatically had repudiated a state attempt to thwart national authority. "America," he wrote, "has chosen to be, in many respects, and to many purposes, a nation; and for all these purposes her government is complete; to all these objects it is competent." A decade later, however, the spectacle of South Carolina's attempt at nullification mocked his words. Marshall was bewildered and disbelieving. He found it "extraordinary . . . that such a question should be seriously debated." Writing to his kindred spirit, Joseph Story, in November 1833, his pessimistic mood then resembled his earlier response to Shays' Rebellion in 1787: "The political world, at least our part of it, is surely moved *topsy turvy.* What is to become of us and of our constitution?"

Marshall's note of despair was, of course, well-founded. His periodic trips to Virginia, as well as his observations of the political scene in Washington, gave him ample opportunity to gauge the growing sentiment for disunion. The fight over the tariff that generated nullification only masked the deeper division over slavery. The Marshall Court generally managed to avoid substantive issues of slavery, particularly when the rulings would have required a determination of constitutionality. "I am not fond of butting against a wall in sport," Marshall told Story at one point. An active member of the American Colonization Society, the chief justice thought colonization the only feasible solution. Colonization proved un-workable, however, and Marshall's successors labored mightily to find a resolution of the slavery controversy within the four corners of the Constitution. Their failure, coupled with the inability of the political system to effectively settle the bitter sectional division, resulted in secession.

The splitting of the Union and the consequent civil war made Marshall's work, in an immediate sense, futile and wasted. The chaos and anarchy of the Confederation that so often haunted him had come full circle. Yet, in the 1860s, the sentiment and necessity for maintenance of the Union belied Marshall's forebodings. Abraham Lincoln's refusal to tolerate secession, instead, sustained the chief justice's conception of constitutionalism. "The people made the constitution, and the people can unmake it," Marshall had said in *Cohens* v. *Virginia*. But, he added, "this supreme and irresistible power to make or unmake resides only in the whole body of the people; not in any subdivision of it." Lincoln's leadership and superior northern power vindicated Marshall. And since the Civil War, time, as Oliver Wendell Holmes said, has been on Marshall's side. Though most of his formal opinions do not concern us today, Marshall left a rich legacy of purpose and meaning for the American Constitution. His contributions to its development and vitality have far transcended his own time and place. "They are destined to enlighten, instruct, and convince future generations," Story predicted in 1833, "and can scarcely perish but with the memory of the constitution itself."

Bibliographical Note

Any reference to John Marshall must begin with *A Bibliography of John Marshall* compiled by James A. Servies (Washington, D.C., 1956). The work was prepared for the United States Commission for the Celebration of the Two Hundredth Anniversary of the Birth of John Marshall. It is conveniently divided into two parts—one, a year-by-year listing of Marshall's known writings, letters, and opinions, and the other, a compilation of contemporary and historical writings on Marshall. Almost as indispensable are the monumental works by Albert Beveridge and Charles Warren. Beveridge's *The Life of John Marshall*, 4 vols. (Boston, Mass., 1916–1919) represents the classic biography. The research is wide-ranging, as is the subject matter; it is, also, a literary masterpiece. Unfortunately, it is flawed by an anti-Jefferson bias that is as unreasoning as Jefferson's dislike of Marshall. Beveridge's depiction of the early national period as a constant duel between Jefferson and Marshall is an exaggeration and distortion of the time and the men. Warren's *The Supreme Court in United States History*, 3 vols. (Boston, Mass., 1922), also has a Federalist bias, yet is immensely valuable for understanding the Court's role and impact. Edward S. Corwin, *John Marshall and the Constitution* (New Haven, Conn., 1919), presents a useful, succinct overview.

Marshall's judicial opinions, both on the Supreme Court and the circuit court, are readily available in most libraries. Extant copies of his correspondence, however, are widely scattered in numerous collections. Some have been published, the most important being a group addressed to Joseph Story and contained in *Proceedings of the Massachusetts Historical Society* 14, 2d ser. (Boston, 1900): 320–60, and Charles Warren, "The Story-Marshall Correspondence (1819–1831)," *William & Mary Quarterly* 21, 2d ser. (1941): 1–26. Some very revealing letters are offered in Jack L. Cross, ed., "John

Marshall on the French Revolution and American Politics," *William & Mary Quarterly* 12, 3d ser. (1955): 631–40. Letters from Marshall to his wife are in Frances Mason, *My Dearest Polly* (Richmond, Va., 1961), and a briefer number in *William & Mary Quarterly* 3, 2d ser. (1923): 73–90. John Oster, *The Political and Economic Doctrines of John Marshall* (New York, 1914) probably offers the largest published collection, but on the whole, the editing is unreliable. Marshall's papers at present are being edited at the Institute for Early American History in Williamsburg under the direction of Stephen Kurtz and Herbert Johnson. A most valuable guide to Marshall's writings is Irwin S. Rhodes, *The Papers of John Marshall: A Descriptive Calendar,* 2 vols. (Norman, Okla., 1970).

Since the publication of the Servies bibliography, there have been a number of significant writings. Robert K. Faulkner, *The Jurisprudence of John Marshall* (Princeton, N.J., 1968), is a fresh treatment, focusing on Marshall as a Lockean liberal. W. Melville Jones, ed., *Chief Justice John Marshall: A Reappraisal* (Ithaca, N.Y., 1956), has several distinguished articles. R. Kent Newmyer, *The Supreme Court Under Marshall and Taney* (New York, N.Y., 1968), offers a splendid synthesis, emphasizing the continuity of judicial and legal history. James Willard Hurst, *Law and the Conditions of Freedom in the Nineteenth Century United States* (Madison, Wis., 1956) and Perry Miller, *The Life of the Mind in America from the Revolution to the Civil War* (New York, N.Y., 1965) stress, respectively, the social and intellectual context of legal development.

Several of Marshall's opinions have been examined in depth. C. Peter Magrath, *Yazoo: Law and Politics in the Early Republic* (Providence, R. I., 1966) is excellent. Donald O. Dewey, *Marshall versus Jefferson: The Political Background of Marbury v. Madison* (New York, N.Y., 1970) also is very good, but it does not examine the impact of the case so well as Magrath's study. Gerald Gunther, ed., *John Marshall's Defense of McCulloch v. Maryland* (Stanford, Calif., 1969) carefully reprints Marshall's anonymously published debate with Spencer Roane. Gunther's introduction is important. Joseph C. Burke, "The Cherokee Cases: A Study in Law, Politics, and Morality," *Stanford Law Review* 21 (1969): 500–531 offers some new insights. Marshall's handling of the treason question is thoroughly explored in James Willard Hurst, *The Law of Treason in the United States: Collected Essays* (Westport, Conn., 1971) and in Bradley Chapin, *The American Law of Treason: Revolutionary and Early National Origins* (Seattle, Wash., 1964). An excellent study of Marshall's relations with his colleagues is Donald M. Roper, "Judicial Unanimity and the Marshall Court—A Road to Reappraisal," *American Journal of Legal History* 9: 118–34 (1965). There have been two fine studies of Marshall's associates: Donald G. Morgan, *Justice William Johnson: The First Dissenter* (Columbia, S.C., 1954) and Gerald Dunne, *Joseph Story* (New York, N.Y., 1971).

The politics surrounding the judiciary from 1800 to 1802 have received extensive attention. Richard Ellis, *The Jeffersonian Crisis: Courts and Politics in the Young Republic* (New York, N.Y., 1971) explores the subject on both the national and state levels. Ellis uses the problem of judicial reform as a vehicle for a new interpretation of the Jeffersonian ascendancy. Dumas Malone's *Jefferson the President, 1801–1805* (Boston, Mass., 1970), the fourth volume of his Jefferson biography, also devotes much attention to the judiciary. Finally, Katherine Turner's articles are indispensable: "The Midnight Judges," *University of Pennsylvania Law Review* 109 (1961): 494–523; "The Appointment of Chief Justice Marshall," *William & Mary Quarterly* 17, 3d ser. (1960): 143–63; and "Federalist Policy and the Judiciary Act of 1801," *Ibid.* 22 (1965): 3–32. The latter conclusively demonstrates that the Federalists considered the expansion of jurisdiction as important as creating new courts.

Index

A

Adams, John, 4, 5, 6, 8, 19, 21, 22, 42, 115, 116, 131
Adams, John Quincy, 6, 91, 115–17
Alien and Sedition Acts, 4, 5, 96–98
American Colonization Society, 172–73
Ames, Fisher, 130
Articles of Confederation, 23–41 passim, 66, 84

B

Baldwin, Henry, 137
Bank of United States v. Dandridge (12 Wheaton 64 [1827]), 147
Bankruptcy, 78–80
Barron v. Baltimore (7 Peters 243 [1833]), 63–66
Beveridge, Albert, 132–33, 134, 142, 144
Bill of Rights, 63–66
Blackstone's Commentaries, 1
Briscoe v. Bank of Kentucky (8 Peters 121 [1837]), 171
Burr trial, 91, 102–3, 116

C

Cabot, George, 5
Carter v. Carter Coal Co. (298 U.S. 238 [1936], 140
Charters and franchises. (See Contract clause)
Chase, Samuel, 102
Chisholm v. Georgia (2 Dallas 419 [1793]), 7
Civil War, 173

Cohens

Cohens v. Virginia (6 Wheaton 264 [1821]), 47–54, 107–13, 135, 136, 153, 172, 173
Commerce clause, 84–90, 152–54
Contract clause, 66–84
Corwin, Edward S., 134–42, 169–70
Crosskey, William W., 143–57

D

Dartmouth College v. Woodward (4 Wheaton 517 [1819]), 73–78, 81, 91
Dred Scott case (19 Howard 393 [1857]), 139

E

Eakin v. Raub (12 Serg. & Rawle [Penna.] 330 [1825]), 163–70 passim
Ellsworth, Oliver, 6, 22

F

Faulkner, Robert K., 157–70
Federal judicial power, 42–54, 107–13
Fiske, John, 138
Fletcher v. Peck (6 Cranch 87 [1810]), 8–11, 66–73, 158
Fuller, Melville, 140
Fulton, Robert, 84

G

Gallatin, Albert, 10
Genet, Edmond, 18
Gerry, Elbridge, 20